# FOUNDATIONS TO LEAD FROM

QUESTIONS THAT WILL TRANSFORM HOW YOU THINK,
FEEL AND LEAD YOUR BUSINESS.

LEIGH HOWES

*authors*
AND CO.

# CONTENTS

# PREFACE

I have always been a dreamer. In the words of Van Gogh, "I dream my painting, and then I paint my dream."

I left a successful HR career in a Fortune500 when I was five months pregnant with our second child, Charlie. Behind my departure was a dream and a point to prove that it was possible to work part time without sacrificing an income and career.

However, like many who transition from a career to running a business, I dived headfirst into 'doing'. Honestly, I winged it. Despite years of working in leadership, considering myself operationally and commercially savvy, I made a multitude of screw ups. It was a roller coaster of cashflow ups and downs, I didn't have the freedom I craved, and for the most part it didn't make me happy. In fact, instead of living out my dream, it almost destroyed me.

A series of difficult personal events and a life-threatening illness in 2017 became my catalyst to positive change. My world imploded and I had one of my biggest 'enough is enough' moments. It was further validation of what needed to change in my business so that I could do more of what made me happy in my life.

I understand what it feels like to be talented but stuck and frustrated. I know there may be missing pieces in your jigsaw too and I want to help you short cut my mistakes and lead a business that makes you money, brings you joy and enables you to feel fulfilled and achieve your dream(s).

In this book, I will ask questions to help you reflect on and review where you are currently and where you want to be. I will also share practical advice, insight and knowledge so you can dig out your business foundations and design a business model that works for you.

As I gently nudge you along the journey, I aim to plant a seed to challenge your thinking about leadership in your business. I am on a mission to change the landscape and create the next generation of CEO. I would love you to be part of it with me.

In this busy, crazy world, I know this to be true: you have the greatest opportunity in your hands to evolve as a leader and grow business your way. Let today be the day you make the decision to take the first step to change, irrespective of the stage your business is at right now.

I thank you for walking this journey with me and look forward to seeing you on the other side.

*Leigh*

*x*

*This book is a combination of my personal and professional journey which includes over 2 decades' experience partnering with business leaders to improve performance, as well as extensive investment in mentors, coaches and educators, alongside knowledge from personal and accredited studying in coaching, business, performance and leadership. In the reference section, you will find some of those who have contributed to my knowledge and this book.*

# INTRODUCTION

---

**"The only person you are destined to become is the person you decide to be."**

— RALPH WALDO EMERSON

---

It has never been easier to start a business. Done right, leading a business is an incredible opportunity to spread your wings and smash through the stifling box of employment. Greater joy, wealth, impact, growth, legacy and time freedom are just some of the incredible benefits of running your own show.

However, whilst it may be easy to get the ship in the water, keeping it there to sail the stormy seas is a whole other ball game. Once the novelty of 'being your own boss' wears off, navigating the waves can be a lonely and overwhelming experience.

Many, like me, dive straight in from a successful career, full of optimism and energy, and wing it. This approach can take you a fair distance, but over time cracks will start to show. Business becomes wobbly as you struggle to find clients, then have too many clients and not enough time. You work too many hours, feel the worry of cashflow and begin to question why you started this journey in the first place. In fact, many of those who are unintentional with their foundations, leadership and strategy find themselves earning less and working more hours than they did when they were employed. I know because I have been there. It sucks.

I want to encourage you to open your mind to the leader your business needs you to be whilst laying foundations that enable you to achieve the success that you define. During our time together, we will explore a series of questions whilst walking you through my Foundation Framework (see figure 1). When you embrace your role as a leader and create more alignment in your business, you create more opportunity for personal and professional growth whilst having a positive impact on others through your work.

# Figure 1 – Foundation Framework™

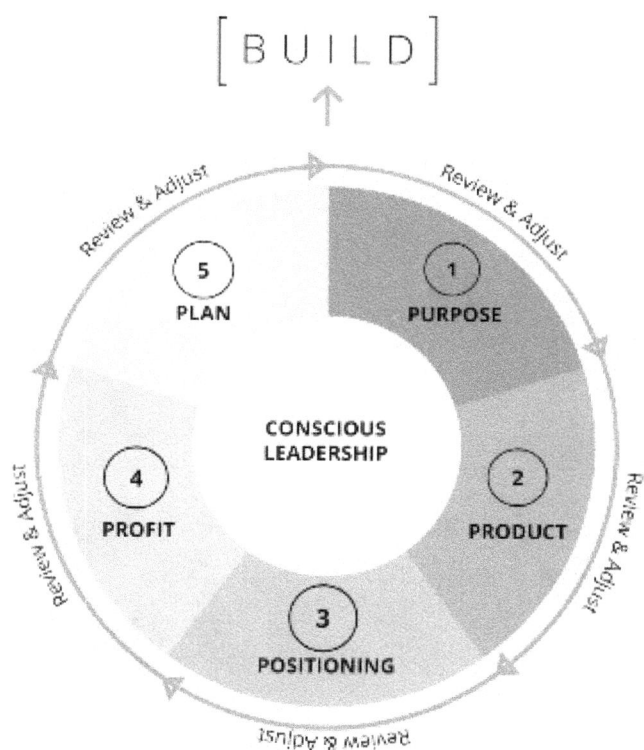

A new generation of CEO is rising in this fast paced, tech-driven world and I would love you to become one of them alongside me.

# HOW TO GET THE MOST OUT OF
# THIS BOOK

---

**"If you don't like where you are – change. You are not a tree."**

— JIM ROHN

---

Before we dive in, I'd like to highlight something important.

Consuming the content of this book (as with any self-study) is just one part of the journey. The critical step is what you do with the insight you gather. The action you take will always be the difference between progress and none.

This book aims to plant a seed and challenge your thinking. But it will only be worth your time if you take intentional action thereafter.

Ask anyone who knows me and they will tell you I am infinitely curious (some may say nosy). Throughout my career, I have seen great opportunities arise for those who are open to different, who challenge the status quo and seek to understand before diving into a solution. I believe in the power of great questions and reflection to get to the root of what you may or may not realise is happening.

As we dive in together, I want you to imagine we are sitting face to face across a table. Imagine I am asking you these questions and providing insight to help you discover your chosen next steps.

I urge you to use the book as a reference tool; make scribbles, highlight key points and fill it with post its. The scruffier it looks, the happier I am for you.

Whilst our time together will focus predominately on the foundations of leadership and business, it will also encourage and give you permission to set up and do things your way. I advocate doing more of what makes you happy and this means leading a business that fits your life and brings joy to it first and foremost. I would place my bet that your definition of success includes how many moments of happiness you can create along the journey. Your business plays a massive part in this. I make no apologies for encouraging you to dig deep to find this insight so you can lay the right foundations for your business, designed your way.

## - Reflective Practice -

As you progress through this book, I will prompt you to reflect on yourself, your current situation and your vision for the future. Reflective practice will help you day-to-day to become more conscious and to develop new skills and insights. It will help you respond better to challenges, make better decisions, manage your emotions better, have more productive relationships, become aware of triggers and cope with stress. Reflective Practice is different from reflection on its own; reflective practice is captured and expressed in some form (written, spoken or pictorial) and is done systematically. When done this way it becomes a habitual activity, and patterns and connections become visible to you on your development journey.

To support this practice, (if you don't already), I recommend grabbing a notebook specifically for our work together (you might also fancy a highlighter and some post it notes too). Use the notebook to journal your reflections as you go through. I have notepads in my bedside drawer, on the coffee table and in my car. I am always listening to my mind and capturing thoughts and ideas, beliefs and patterns. Reflective practice is a brilliant tool to help you start to become more self-aware and is an equally brilliant way to capture those important insights and ideas that may come to mind too.

As you navigate the book, you will see areas marked as REFLECTIONS. These are meant to prompt you to stop, think, respond and plan your actions. I know how busy you are, so where possible, I encourage you to respond to these as you read. You might want to use your highlighter to capture the actions you propose or any lightbulb moments.

That said, I have written the book so that you can go back and pick out the question you need when you need it. This means you can digest it in one hit, pick it up and read it slowly or use it as a reference tool when your foundations need a review.

When using your notepad to capture your reflections either in the moment or after, this is a useful process to follow.

**Reflection in Action**

Relive the experience. What exactly happened? How did you feel? Notice the patterns – thoughts, feelings, physical responses as they happen or when you relive it. What else can you learn about yourself, your triggers and reactions? What other insights did you gather?

**Next Steps**

Once you have gathered this information, how can you reframe and look at it objectively? What steps can you take next to move forward? What needs to change for next time? What do you need to look out for?

# THE NEXT GENERATION OF CEO

**Let's talk about the elephant in the room.**

**It is highly probable that you (like many of my clients before our work together) don't see yourself as a leader or CEO of your business right now.**

**I would love to open your mind to a different perspective.**

Let's back up a bit.

In definition terms, within a traditional business structure the CEO is the highest job title or rank. This role and its responsibilities are open to wide interpretation. It is fair to say that most perceive the title as only relevant to leaders of bigger companies with a large team and shareholders to answer to.

Alongside those that don't resonate, I have also witnessed mocking in the wider business world of the so-called 'gravitas' of using the title CEO when you run the operation alone.

Let me be frank. The CEO is like much of our business world, changing. Go into the fastest growing start-ups and you'll see a variety of set ups and leaders. They may be hot seating in their open plan office in trainers and a hoody or leading a largely online business from their garden office. Perhaps they do have a big team in an office or they may work with a lean team from an office at their home. Or they could be suited in a plush board room or running their operation from a sun lounger as they travel the world and run their business remotely.

My point is, if you are put off by the title because you see a CEO as 'a suited male in a big office surrounded by a large team and answering to shareholders' - you are missing my point. I use and refer to CEO not for the title, but to highlight the actions, behaviours and mindset that the key decision maker within your business will need to develop to support its success. You can be the CEO (or whatever title) of your choosing, wear what you want, work where you want, when you want and how you want. But it is critical to understand the key components of being the leader and CEO of your business, because as you grow, your actions could make or break its success.

### I run my business alone or with a small team... how does that work?

A CEO is typically responsible for the success or failure of a business and is its key decision maker. Depending on the business set up, structure and size, this responsibility could include overseeing operations, marketing, strategy, financing, company culture, human resources, compliance, sales, PR, communications and IT. It all falls on the CEO's shoulders directly or indirectly (although as a business grows, the CEO would not necessarily lead these functions, but have leaders or team in place instead). Some business owners also choose to hire in a CEO further down the line whilst they take on a different role as they recognise their skill set isn't a fit. You will need to figure out the right approach for you as your business grows.

For the purpose of this book (and for most of the owner managed businesses I support), the majority will choose to take on the role of CEO themselves.

When you own the business (especially when you are a personal brand), it is likely that your natural emotional attachment to it will at times impact your judgement, boundaries and the actions that you do or don't take. This takes adjustment when you have transitioned from employment. In employment to someone else you are able to detach the emotion, whereas you immerse yourself so much into your own business that sometimes it can be more difficult to do.

To help you overcome this, I encourage you to build your awareness of when this may be happening, and to start to step back and aim to become more objective. Acknowledge that you may be making decisions based too much on emotion; ask yourself, **'What would a CEO do right now?'**

By asking yourself this important question, you allow yourself to look at your business through another perspective.

To help you open your mind, I have explored below what I see as the responsibilities of this role in an owner managed business: -

1. Setting strategy and direction. Knowing the answers to 'where are you going?' and 'how?' are important. This is the most important responsibility of a CEO in a company of any size. In the absence of someone to

lead your operations, you will need to ensure that your execution is as strong as your vision. This can be challenging if your bias is in idea generation and not in implementation.

2. Clarity on your target audience (otherwise known as your ideal client) and how you will attract them through your sales and marketing activities. As well as the components of your business model (product mix and pricing), one of the most important activities for you is developing your sales, marketing and distribution channels that you use to build up your audience. This is often one of the hardest nuts to crack for the owner managed business. It is always better to have too many of the right leads to convert than not enough. You will need to invest time and develop your skills in these areas or invest money and hire in someone to do this for you.

3. Modelling and setting your company culture, purpose, mission, values and behaviour are important so that you build a business that fits your needs and the needs of those that you hire. Alignment to this gives maximum joy, fulfilment and satisfaction. You may not hire a team immediately, but you will want to create a great environment so you can attract and retain high performers and clients and be seen as a brand and employer of choice. As you build and position your brand, this work is important both internally and externally to build trust and loyalty. Don't try and be someone you are not – you will get caught out.

4. Building and leading a team. I advocate surrounding yourself with others who have strengths you do not. Whilst you may not be in a position to hire immediately, I recommend you consider early on

where you can bring in team member(s) to help with the gaps/holes in your boat, so you can leverage your time and focus on what you love to do best. Whilst I advocate taking *informed* risks, I do recommend bringing in your first hire before you feel ready: it will make the growth phase of your business more fluid and viable. I would add that if you get creative, hiring is much more accessible in the early days than most business owners fully appreciate.

5. Allocating and overseeing financials is a priority for a CEO. Financials MUST be taken seriously. You are dangerously winging it if you have your head in the sand and focus only on your end of year tax return or quarterly VAT bill. The CEO should set and allocate budgets and be responsible for reviewing and adjusting spend accordingly. Whilst you might not consider yourself financially focused, it is your decisions that determine the financial success of the company. Therefore, it is imperative that you develop your financial acumen and systems or hire someone early on to do it for you.

Building a successful business isn't going to be easy. I speak from personal experience when I tell you (if you haven't discovered it already) that it will test and challenge you. There are many who don't make it through the initial stages of getting up and running and others that barely make enough to pay themselves. Conversely, when set up right and in alignment to your values, needs and joy (more on this to follow) the opportunities and rewards can be more than you ever experienced being employed.

Irrespective of whether you are here at the start of your journey (kudos if you are getting the foundations laid from day one – I wish I had!) or if you are on your journey but looking to draw a line and stop winging it, it is fair to say, we have some work to do together.

What got you to this point won't necessarily get you to the next level. Greater growth comes when you move away from being the team member (aka employee), leverage your strengths and look at bringing in support to free up your time. Whilst it may not happen immediately, if you want more time and more money, you will need to look at things differently.

# YOUR LEAP

---

**"The comfort zone is the great enemy of courage and confidence."**

— BRIAN TRACY

---

I would like to take a few minutes to speak with you about taking leaps. I would be lying if I said that leading a business into growth will be comfortable for you.

Leaps often come from trauma, crisis and 'enough is enough' moments. In other words, the dark gift you didn't ask for but was handed to you anyway.

I know this to be true because at least two of my biggest leaps have been driven by major events in my life. Redundancy and Cancer.

## *Why do we wait until it is raining to fix our roof?*

I will tell you why. Fear of the unknown and because it is safe and comfortable to stay where you are right now.

But under the comfort of that safety blanket, you can have itchy, fidgeting feet. You get frustrated. There is a part of the jigsaw that doesn't quite fit or is missing altogether.

Gay Hendricks in his book *The Big Leap* talks about operating in one of four zones.

- Incompetence
- Competence
- Excellence
- Genius

**The zone of incompetence** is self-explanatory. You are not great at X and someone else would be able to do it better than you.

**The zone of competence** is when you can do something, but someone else could do it as well or better/quicker than you.

Meanwhile, **in your zone of genius** you leverage your strengths (your energy is high and you love it so much it doesn't feel like work) and you are brilliant at it too – **this is your happy place**!

However, over in **your zone of excellence**, you are equally brilliant. Your clients love you there - you get a heap of recognition for your work, but you no longer love it. You may have loved it once, but the fire has burnt out (or is starting to fade.) It leaves your energy low and makes it feel like you are running through treacle some days. However, it is safe, you are comfortable and to move into your zone of genius would be a **BIG** (if not quantum) LEAP. This is where many get stuck.

A wonderful client of mine is a brilliant example of being in your zone of excellence. She was a well-known authority in her field, brilliant at what she delivered. She received a heap of recognition for her results and impact. But her model and way of working had a massive impact on her personal life. She would find herself working into the weekend when she really wanted to be with her family. She was often on duty, feeling stressed and overwhelmed, and the spark that was once there was flickering, about to go out. Through our initial work together, she became more conscious of the work that lit her up, her core strengths, and found she wasn't doing enough of this day-to-day. However, she was firmly sat in her zone of excellence; numbers were great, profit was positive. To change would take a big leap of courage.

There is a difference between waiting for a crisis to make the leap and deciding to grab the reins and make the leap yourself. I am pleased to report that she courageously took hold of those reins, made some initial baby steps forward and then took the big leap in a revised direction. She now has a model that allows much more room to scale without working more hours. All of this enables her to be more present with her family, take more time off, and have fewer (and the right) clients whom she is helping get great results. She has increased her prices and profit. Most importantly, she is doing more of what makes her happy.

But she first had to be willing to change. She had to decide enough was enough and have a big vision of what she wanted her life to look like and find the courage and willingness to set about the actions to make the leap. Was it easy? No! There were doubts and wobbles along the way. But she has made the leap and I am beyond excited about the next chapter for her.

Perhaps you resonate? Maybe you are just getting started or don't believe you have the revenue to hire someone into your team. So, you carry on doing ALL the things alone.

You spend a chunk of time working in your zone of incompetence or competence creating graphics, financials, social media posts or copy. Yet your passion and sales come from the conversations you create. You are brilliant here and love to develop new leads and create new opportunities. But your time and energy are zapped in areas that take you away from the revenue generating activities that could massively improve the performance of your business. The crazy thing is you could probably hire someone for a minimal amount and they could create your graphics, financials, social media posts or copy, leaving you to focus on your zone of genius and source a new client while they take care of the rest.

Perhaps you are in a job and hustling on the side with the business venture that you desperately want to leap into. You need a certain amount of cashflow to make the leap viable, but the goalposts keep moving and the time never seems right. Sometimes it isn't about the viability of the numbers adding up. Sometimes it is about having the courage to be willing to change, to stop resisting, step out of the safety of your zone of excellence and make the leap.

## Reflections

**Using your notepad, capture your reflections.**

1. Where could you be working right now in your business in your zone of incompetence and wasting precious time (and sending yourself stir crazy)? If you delegated this, how would it free up your time? If you cannot hire in immediately, how integral is this to your business right now?
2. Where are you stuck and feeling drained in the zone of competence or excellence? Where do you know that you could add more value and get greater joy elsewhere?
3. What do you love to do that would help you make that leap into your zone of genius? What would you love to become more courageous at doing?

## My Leaps

I consider that I started my career when I took a role as an office manager within a Recruitment Company.

I had a blank sheet of paper. An opportunity to implement what I had learned during my studies. Equally, this is when I realised that challenging the status quo and my non-conformity (done respectfully) could serve me well. The consultancy was primarily focused on senior sales roles within the housewares and textile industry. When an opportunity to recruit telesales people arose (small fee, high volume) the senior recruiters were unimpressed by the opportunity. So I volunteered. I proudly (and not so humbly) report that I did a great job and my love of 'people' and leadership was born.

I was told I had the potential to move into what was then known as personnel. I immediately shook my head. My experience of this was grey skirts, flat shoes, people stopping you doing what you wanted (hire and fire was my stereotype). I also had a massive fear of public speaking. The person in question encouraged me to open my eyes and consider it. This is the power of someone believing in you before you do.

I enrolled on a foundation course called the CPP (Certificate in Personnel Practice). To say I loved it was an understatement. I soaked up my new learning experience and, despite my fear, embraced the terror of public speaking and started to grow in confidence. I then took a gamble and applied for a job as a Recruitment Officer with Iceland Frozen Foods. When I got it, nobody was more shocked (or terrified) than me.

Overnight, I went from having a ten-minute drive to work in my much loved but tatty Nova, to choosing a brand-new company car and managing the recruitment of Iceland's Appliance Sales Managers, living out of a suitcase as I travelled all over the UK. I officially stepped into my first leadership role at a young age when I recruited a small team to support me. My First BIG leap!

I had a speedy upward trajectory from there - moving into a HR business partner role with the Area Operations team, then a Regional Partner Role partnering with the Regional Operations team and leading the HR Business Partners in my region. It was whilst doing this that I decided to study for the degree that I hadn't fancied doing at university.

Thereafter, I was headhunted to work with the well-known brand, KFC (part of Yum Restaurants International – a Fortune500 company). I spent nine years there, starting in a Regional HR Operations role before being promoted into Head Office to head up HR there, supporting the Board under the guidance of the VP of HR.

The BIG leaps scared the bejesus out of me. But every time I leapt, I saw a shift in my energy, hunger, growth and stretch. I had countless voices in my head, doubting me and I had to compartmentalise to manage the overwhelm that these big leaps threw my way. But I continued to invest in my development as I knew this was vital for my performance to continue to improve.

In 2009, our first child, Henry, was born. Up until this point, I was a work horse. Often the last one in the office, I was climbing the ladder and loved my work with a passion.

But when Henry arrived, I changed. Whilst my hunger to work and desire to develop hadn't changed, my priorities had. I knew that the way I had been working before wasn't going to be possible moving forward. This was a really difficult time for me.

Reducing my work to four days in my current head of HR role wasn't viable, so I accepted a HR Project Role which was created for me. This saw me leading an important recruitment project to source high performing talent for the operational team.

But I wasn't the same person when I returned. I had the same skills, worked as hard, was as committed, but in all honesty, I had changed. It wasn't that I didn't enjoy it, I just couldn't sit in my office until 8.30pm to meet a deadline. I had someone at home that needed me more.

One of the pivotal 'enough is enough' moments for me was during a two-day offsite meeting with the HR leadership team. Ordinarily I would have loved this time away, getting strategic and building the relationships offsite. We were in a beautiful hotel in the countryside, no expense spared. Instead, I was calling home, missing Grahame and Henry. I was listening to the conversations and feeling like I no longer fitted in. The misalignment was horrendous.

In the afternoon, we had to present our plans for the next twelve months. I fell apart. Midway through, the tears started to fall. I was mortified. I had never cried at work. Not only did I feel unprofessional, I felt like a failure. I excused myself and ran to the toilet. After a while, I brushed myself down, returned to the meeting and the elephant in the room wasn't discussed. When I look back now, this was one of the very first 'enough is enough' moments for me. Change was afoot.

Not long after, I was approached to move across to our sister brand, Pizza Hut, on secondment. They needed someone to work alongside their Managing Director and Operations Director. I would head up HR in the delivery team and manage the refranchising of their sites. Not only a great opportunity but their Head Office was located just forty minutes from my home.

From the minute I moved, I felt like me again. The team were wonderful, the pressure of travel was no more and as a result my happiness and confidence returned. I was back to my old self, managing the balance of work and family.

In April 2011, I became aware that I couldn't do this indefinitely. It was a secondment. There were lots of changes in the business and I needed to think about what I was going to do next.

It was at this stage I dipped my toe into working for myself. I discovered an industry that would go on to be a huge catalyst to my change - 'Network Marketing'. I honestly didn't understand how it all worked, I just got enthused by the model. It was here that I started my first side hustle alongside the day job.

In February 2012, after changes within the business and a reluctance to step backwards due to a lack of part time opportunities, I took redundancy.

I started to look for work. I was highly regarded for roles. There was lots of interest in me and my experience. However, no one would consider me working four days a week. It was either full time or no time.

I found myself unwilling to accept this reality. It was at this stage that my vision became clear. It was born from what I wanted of my life first and foremost. My vision was and continues to be one of freedom and choice. I have made it my mission to prove that I and others could look after a family and still build a profitable business our way.

So, at five months pregnant with our second child, Charlie, I took redundancy without a job to go to and decided I would throw myself into working for myself.

**On reflection, I have gained many learnings and insights. As part of your reflection practice, you might find it useful to look back over your career to date and consider your big leaps. Sometimes you don't realise they even happened until you reflect on them.**

## Your Transferrable Skills

In conjunction with your leaps are your skills and those you may need to develop.

Business owners like you come to me frustrated, sometimes with a lack of clients, sometimes with masses of overwhelm. When I peel the onion, here is what I find.

Like mine, your business started because of a desire for something different or because of dissatisfaction. Maybe you are running a business that relates to an existing set of skills from employment. Perhaps you were a lawyer and now provide legal counsel and support to small business owners. Or like me, you worked in HR and now provide consultancy and coaching services to business leaders. Or perhaps you have moved completely away from your career and are turning that much loved passion and hobby into a business.

Please know this. Just because you were incredible in your previous career and have a heap of transferrable skills, it doesn't mean you ALREADY know how to lead a business. Conversely, because you don't know how to lead a business it doesn't mean you are not brilliant, talented and capable of making a difference to others through the work you do. Please read this paragraph again. I need you to KNOW and BELIEVE this.

Employment typically means you focus on one specialism in your role. Leading a business requires you to have a broad skill set in areas you may never have worked in before. Therefore, unless you hire others in to do it for you, you will need to learn new skills, open your mind to change and develop your leadership and business acumen as you continue to leverage those incredible transferrable skills of yours.

Don't let the difficulties of leading your business impact the belief in your abilities to make a difference through your work. Becoming a CEO requires you to get super curious and aware of your strengths and limitations and in time it will likely mean you will need to hire in others who are brilliant at the stuff you are not – and that is OK!

## Reflections

1. What can you learn from your big leaps?
2. What did you feel in those moments?
3. What were the triggers and patterns when you reflect on them?
4. What can you learn from them about how you think and behave today in your work/life?
5. What do you notice has changed or needs to?

## Your Self-Belief

Self-belief (or self-efficacy) is a person's belief in their ability to complete tasks and to achieve their goals (Bandura, 1995). Judging yourself to be capable of success increases your chance of actual success. Judging yourself as not capable of success reduces the chance of success.

Self-belief means that you should have enough self-confidence to change, but not that you over-estimate your abilities, as that could in turn become a fixed mindset attitude.

A person with self-belief knows their worth and value. They are more likely to take a chance and go after the sale, show up more in their marketing, develop themselves as a leader and grow their business. They explore what is possible and push for further growth because they believe they have what it takes to make it happen.

A person lacking self-belief will downplay their abilities and settle for less than their true potential because it is less risky. In extreme cases, someone lacking self-belief could make less than sensible choices and accept negative or unacceptable behaviour towards them that doesn't align to their values or that pushes their boundaries because they don't believe they deserve better.

The result is that the person becomes frustrated because they are letting opportunities pass them by, they feel overwhelmed because they cannot say no, they don't ask for help and may not be charging enough for their services because they don't see why anyone would pay what they are truly worth.

This shows that while self-belief might seem inconsequential to those who have it, it can affect life and work, directly and indirectly.

Self-belief motivates you to explore your potential and this in turn creates opportunity for growth, fulfilment and happiness. The ingredient a leader is often missing when up levelling performance is the belief that they can achieve it in the first place.

At *Yum!* we referred to a **PUSH and PULL formula - M=bp2.**

It works on the principle that your motivation to act comes from = **Believability x Pleasure x Pain.**

We shouldn't underestimate the power of our beliefs. Our beliefs impact our thoughts, emotions, energy and in turn our physical body and reality. Henry Ford once famously said, 'Whether you think you can or you can't, you are right.'

To motivate yourself to BIG action, you need to start with believing you can do it. If you don't believe, you will only 'try'. You'll use language like *I need* and *I should* as you procrastinate and avoid taking action. Look for the signs; this is where your reflective practice will serve you well.

Belief is multiplied by

> The PULL of a goal (and the pleasure associated with accomplishing it) x The PUSH of being dissatisfied with how things are (and the pain associated with staying as you are)

---

**"Do or do not, there is no try."**

— YODA

---

I know and believe that action really does cure the fear - it stretches the comfort zone and when you are comfortable, you feel confident. Sometimes we need to just do it and kick start the motor to take the step forward.

No one is born without self-belief. Most times, we find ourselves in situations and circumstances that can negatively affect our self-esteem – either temporarily or in the long run.

To rebuild your self-belief, understanding the circumstance that made you lose it can help you learn how to proceed.

Your pattern of self-beliefs can also be reprogrammed. However, to do this requires you first to be willing to change. To become willing to change, you need to understand what you want to change and what makes you resistant to taking the first steps of action to achieve it.

*NOTE: Whilst this work is enough for some, you may need additional, deeper, more targeted support to work through the more subconscious beliefs that block your progress. Please explore this option if you need to.*

# 1

# ARE YOU WILLING TO CHANGE?

---

**"Every challenge that we face is the opportunity
to become more than we've been before."**

— LYENA STRELKOFF

---

If you want different, you got to move differently. Actions speak louder than words and saying you want something doesn't always translate into action. Change requires courage and a willingness to do things differently. It will likely be painful too. You know what they say: 'no pain, no gain'.

As our first question together, I want you to be honest with yourself and ask if you are really willing to change to get a different result. Then, if you are ready. ask what you could do differently to move forward?

## My catalyst to change

Earlier I explained that big leaps often follow trauma or crisis. One of my biggest catalysts to change followed trauma.

---

*"We have had your results back; they are positive."*

---

I stared across the table at the breast consultant. I was momentarily confused. "Positive," I thought, that's got to be good, surely? However, out of my mouth came a very shaky, "What does that mean?" His response.... "I'm afraid it's cancer."

The sentence we all fear. Me included. I sat with my head in my hands, shocked to the core. I had become in that split second a new statistic, a sob story that would be shared amongst others. My heart broke in two.

I was, or so I thought, a healthy 42-year-old, with two boys aged seven and four and a husband who had lost his own father to cancer just two months before.

It felt like a bad dream. I recall shrinking in my seat and shaking. In a voice I didn't recognise as my own, I quietly voiced my thoughts. "Will I die? I cannot die, my boys need me, they are only babies. My husband needs me, he has only just lost his Dad." My head sank forward. Any strength I ever had disappeared in that moment. The consultant looked at me with sympathy; what could he say?

The drive home was strange. My husband, Grahame, quietly sobbed. Hardly surprising considering the battering we had both had over the past few years and everything he had been through over the previous eight months with his own Dad. A strange calm came over me. However, the calm didn't last.

Those of you reading this who have had life changing moments will know that with them often comes a massive spoonful of perspective, which can give you a 'don't give a f**k' attitude' e.g.- 'best you do it now' as tomorrow isn't guaranteed.

All the things that I thought were important, I realised were just immaterial. All I could think of in those minutes following my diagnosis were my family and it was them that gave me the will to get better.

As I armed myself with the facts, the truth of surgery, chemo-therapy and the immense fear I felt, I knew I needed to find ways to dig deep and find resilience and strength; to get through it and see my little boys grow up.

Over the days that followed, I reflected that for too long, I hadn't been doing enough of what made me happy. I rarely put the oxygen mask on and looked after me first. I had fallen onto the hamster wheel because survival and overwhelm have a habit of taking over without you realising.

Two days after my diagnosis, I turned to one of my childhood friends. She listened, was supportive and generous with her time and expertise as a holistic therapist. She was one of the first people who saw me completely on my knees; her kindness, love, honesty and treatments were a huge part of my healing and remain a big part of the perspective and changes to self-care that enabled (and enable) me to continue to grow from the trauma that I found myself in.

Very early on she asked for permission to be honest. She said, "Leigh, you have had whispers to wake up, then the voices got a little louder and this is the final scream that you need to change. You may not know it now, but one day you will feel able to see this trauma as a gift."

It was a very big wake-up call for me, but honestly, I didn't get it. Why and how was it a gift? But she was right. A dark gift had landed and it was up to me to make something positive out of the shit storm it had stirred up.

## My dream

I started my business in 2012 with little Charlie five months in my tummy and three-year-old Henry. I was full of ambition, drive, hunger, passion, a ton of experience, transferrable skills and my dream (and point to prove) of ambitiously working part time.

I craved freedom and choice since becoming a Mum. I wanted to work how I chose, but without sacrificing a progressive career and revenue. My first financial goal was to replace my prior well-paid full-time income.

But honestly, whilst the dream was strong, the plan to execute it was non-existent. Transitioning from a successful career to running a business, despite the skills I had, wasn't the easiest thing I have ever done. I winged it. I fake smiled and I rode, like many, the feast and famine roller coaster of business ownership.

Prior to cancer, I'd had an earlier 'enough is enough' moment. At two years old, Charlie was taken to hospital in an ambulance very ill with Pneumonia. It was the second week in December 2014 and as anyone with children will appreciate, it was a truly horrendous time. As I slept in a bed by his cot for what felt like eternity, I found myself taking a call from a client for a headhunting assignment I was working on for a big corporate. This client would have happily waited until my son improved. But I was in survival mode. Feast or Famine meant money mattered. I had to land this placement. I sat next to his bed, on the phone talking shop; I realised just how far away I was from my dream of freedom. I was my own boss, but I wasn't free at all.

It was then I made a commitment – I willed Charlie better and promised myself and him I would change things. I was working in complete misalignment to what I wanted for my family. It was no longer an option to continue this way.

Thankfully, a week or so after his admission, Charlie turned a corner and we had him home in time for Christmas.

I resurrected the vision, stepped away from what I had been doing, took a different direction and dived into a different vehicle. I was determined to find a way to leverage and free up my time. 2015 was the year I detoured into the Network Marketing Industry and built up an income that taught me a heap about time leverage, recurring revenue and potential opportunities for putting passive and semi passive products into your business model.

But to cut twelve months of story short, after much investment of time and energy, I learnt it wasn't the right vehicle for me either and the work wasn't always lighting me up. Whilst the experience gave me much insight, excitement and knowledge about an entirely different business model (which has been a godsend for the way I work today), I realised that in my quest to support my developing team, I was working evenings and weekends because that was when they were available. While knee deep in this, I realised I didn't want to work at those times, as this was when I wanted to be with my family. Working in such misalignment was making me unhappy. I was back to whizzing around the hamster wheel. I still didn't have the choices and freedom I craved.

**Here is the thing. Before you work on your ideal client (as you should), you need to decide what is most important to you. If you don't do this, you run the risk of attracting clients who don't align with your own needs and values. Without this important work, you might build a business that you want to run from rather than lead.**

### How can you embrace change?

Change is you stepping into unknown territory. You will likely feel that you release control and there is the possibility of failure.

Your resistance to embracing change is generally rooted in fear.

However, one guarantee in leading your business successfully is that change is a constant.

In a society with technology at the forefront of how we live and work, change is rapid and inevitable. You need to equip yourself with strategies and techniques and arm yourself with resilience and agility to ride the roller coaster of change. At the time of publishing, we are still going through a period of uncertainty after the global pandemic of COVID-19. This period has tested business resilience and agility. It is those who opened their minds, got creative, took ownership and were agile that have survived or in many cases thrived through a harrowing period.

Having a closed and fixed mindset as a leader (more on this in Question 2) will result in you being the bottleneck in your business. I have seen so many amazing business concepts destroyed by the attitude of the key decision maker because they refuse or are scared to get curious, take responsibility and embrace change. This results in a business that stalls and goes stale whilst competitors pick up speed, navigate the journey with agility and speed, and overtake.

Your development as the leader in your business will correlate with its growth and success.

You could invest time and money in updates to systems, learn new ways to work, have a shiny new CRM system and put clear processes in place – but still stand still in the execution.

Your business won't change just because of a new system, new website, new business model, new product or pricing structure. Your business will change when you as the leader (and any team) change with it.

The famous change curve model (which is mostly attributed to psychiatrist, Elisabeth Kubler-Ross) is a well-known, powerful model and reference point. It shows how people generally behave and transition through change and trauma. The model has been adapted over the years since its creation in the 1960s but is a great visual representation in predicting how most react to change.

As the person leading and responsible for the key decisions in your business, how you respond to change will be a key decider as to how well you execute and act on change that is needed as your journey continues.

The original model works through four stages: -

**Stage 1 – Shock or denial** as the status quo is challenged. It is vital at this stage to keep communication open, supportive and honest – keep yourself and your teams fully informed of the facts.

**Stage 2 – Anger, fear, resistance** (the most disruptive and potentially chaotic and unproductive stage). This is when the reality of the change hits home. It will often bring about negativity as emotions range from fear, anger, resistance and sometimes protesting the change or trauma. Sometimes your behaviour will assume the worst and believe only the negatives of the situation. It is critical that emotions at this stage are handled carefully and sensitively. Each person will navigate through at their own pace.

**Stage 3 – Acceptance (exploration).** At this stage you will move from looking at what is lost to accepting the changes. You will likely test, explore and implement some of the early changes and start to see their impact. You are in adaptive mode and this can often be the catalyst for positive change. Whilst you explore, a supportive and honest approach is needed to help you navigate.

**Stage 4 – Commitment (rebuilding).** At this stage, you are accepting the changes and executing any new ideas that have resulted. Only at this stage can the business start to reap the rewards of the change process. Recognition of your progress, reflections on the growth and celebrations of wins and achievements are key to enable you to move forward.

The speed at which you move through each stage depends on several factors – your current state of mind, how much prior trauma or upheaval you have faced, your personal circumstances, tools, strategies and general resilience.

I particularly like this adapted model shared by steemit.com. As someone who has experienced loss not only through the grieving of a loved one, but because of my journey with cancer, I believe the most unsettling stage of managing our emotions to change is the valley of despair. When unknown, we don't have the full facts and it is difficult to explore and move into acceptance without them.

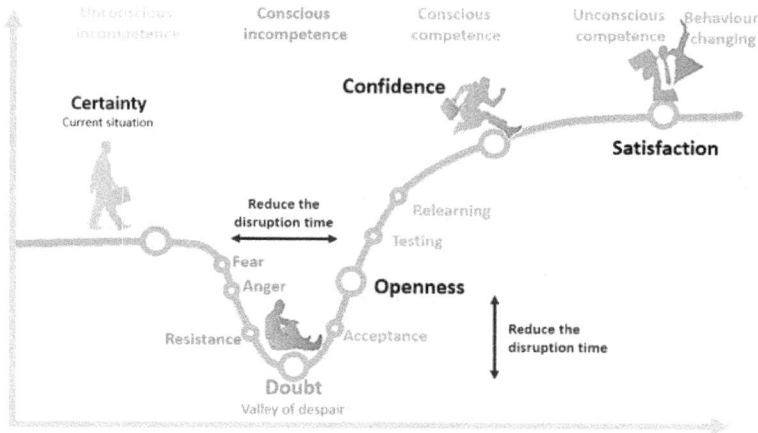

*Source: https://steemit.com/life/@futureentech/the-change-curve-in-our-life-we-can-change-our-journey.*

In my own valley of despair, I was not productive; I found it hard to concentrate, sleep, communicate and even eat. However, as I started to arm myself with the facts and face the reality of my situation, I started to accept and became open to exploring actions to move forward.

This may sound dramatic but is a common feeling when you run your business too. When stretching yourself to reach new goals, you might find yourself simply standing still. Sometimes in this stage, like mine, your behaviours might not serve you or improve your situation. Perhaps you scroll your phone, don't sleep as well, procrastinate, and go round in circles feeling more and more overwhelmed. Your subconscious controls more than 80% of your thoughts and behaviours, so even though consciously you may know you can do something, your subconscious may have other ideas. It wants you to stay safe, to stick with what you know. It doesn't want you to change. When you want to realise your potential and evolve your business and leadership, recognising which voice is controlling you is a huge milestone to attain.

It is also important to note that a call for change often comes easy in the heat of the moment. However, once the fire is out, the call for change may die too. Therefore, the habits, systems, routines that are in place to embed the change are critical for its positive impact to be felt. It was easier when my life was under threat to go all in on my self-care, healing and wellbeing. When the threat was removed, it was easy to slip back into my old ways.

So many people gain perspective through dark times. This perspective is often the catalyst for big and positive change (a big leap) in our lives. How many do something extraordinary after trauma, changing something that they had sat on for years? There are many who have used their perspective to grow through their experience, that otherwise they might never have actioned.

But why? Why does it take the rain to come before you fix the leaky roof? Why not fix the leak before it starts to rain? Why wait until the dark times to create the change you crave?

I have been guilty of this. My 'enough is enough' moments have often been my triggers and catalysts to change.

But whilst it takes a growth mindset to reframe traumatic situations and grow through them – you are still in the passenger seat.

I want to encourage you to get back in the driver's seat. Don't wait until it is raining to take action.

### How can you move differently?

**In the book *15 Commitments of Conscious Leadership*, Jim, Diana and Kaley share a change formula which builds on the one I shared on from my time at *Yum!***

**Credit for this formula goes to Richard Beckhard, David Gleicher and Kathie Dannemiller. You can read it in full in their 2014 edition, page 304.**

The formula which they believe determines the likelihood of change occurring is

$$(V \times D) + FS > R = C$$

They discuss that to bring about change, there must be something for you to focus on that is greater than the resistance you feel.

In this formula, **V = Vision.** This is your picture of a preferable future. If large enough, it can motivate you to face your fears and step through the resistance to act. This is similar to the *Yum!* Formula where the pull of the goal is critical to the motivation to take action.

But for this to work, it cannot be a tick box exercise; it needs to be heartfelt and compelling. My vision of freedom is an example of this. But amongst this I have other elements to my vision.

Security, Legacy, Fulfilment, Choices.

We will dive deeper into your vision and your why in Question 3, but something to ponder for now is:

### How big and compelling is your vision?: How connected do you feel to it?

### D = Dissatisfaction.

Change through vision alone is often not enough. Again, like the *Yum!* Formula this combines the pull (goal and vision) and push (dissatisfaction) to motivate you to act.

An example of this would be during my time in HR. One KPI that Operation Managers were accountable for was team turnover.

When we explored what was driving turnover, Managers would often list 'salary' as the reason.

I regularly challenged this. Having spent many years in focus groups, exit interviews and discussions with both engaged and unengaged teams, a common theme was apparent.

Job searches don't generally start from a place of being under-paid. Providing basic needs are met (as per Maslow's Hierarchy of Needs Model), then this is not what drives a decision for change or action. This drive for change comes when they have overcome the resistance for it and instead feel the pull of some-thing different, together with the dissatisfaction of staying where they are. This is their motivation to commence a job search.

It was the dissatisfaction an employee felt that made the salary a part of the problem. If they were satisfied and fulfilled, the salary was unlikely to be a problem (unless basic needs were not being met).

My point is that most of us can overcome resistance to change when we become dissatisfied with where we are. Sometimes we might not realise this until we start to peel the onion back to explore it. Sometimes we may put our heads in the sand to avoid confronting the dissatisfaction. We pretend it isn't happening but when we shine a light on it, we realise just how impactful it is on our energy and fulfilment.

**FS = First Steps**. These are the baby steps you need to take to start to move into change. When you are at the foot of the mountain and see your vision at the top, it can feel over-whelming to move towards it and resistance therefore is stronger. When you focus on one action (and step) at a time, you will likely feel less resistance and will start to gradually climb without even realising you are making progress upwards.

Remember that confidence is simply operating in your comfort zone. Action helps cure the fear and these first steps are a part of this process to change.

**Vision x Dissatisfaction + First Steps >: becomes greater than resistance and this is what = Change**

In my observations of business owners, sometimes I hear the following words: -

*"I need; I should; I will try."*

*"I would like to change, but I need to know how."*

**"I just need to know how."**

**"I don't know what I need to do."**

Sometimes, of course, you need to know the exact steps.

But often, not knowing 'how' is an excuse. It could be a subconscious decision and you may not even realise it, but it could be that you are in fact unwilling and resisting change, and even knowing the steps wouldn't make you take action.

I will give you an example.

- A client is struggling to get new clients. We discuss the root of the issue and the action that needs to happen to change this.
- It becomes apparent that high touch calls to potential leads is the action that needs to be taken. The client acknowledges that this isn't their favourite activity, but they do not have anyone (or a budget) to delegate the task to. Therefore, if they want more clients, they will have to own the activity and action. They ask for specific details as to how. I show them.
- Two weeks later, the same issue is raised. When I explore what action was taken following our discussion, they say they don't know how. That they need further clarity on what it is they need to do.

I could keep going over this with them and I could pretty much guarantee the same conversation will keep coming up. The issue is not in them not knowing how. The issue is most likely in their willingness or belief to change.

A client once said to me, "I feel like I am in the rowing boat going round and round and I need someone to tell me how to row..." My reply was, "Sometimes even if I show you how to row, the likelihood is your boat will still go round in circles."

This is because even if you are armed with the knowledge of 'how to do something', it doesn't mean you will. This is why there are so business owners addicted to courses and training. Constantly (and non-strategically) chasing the magic formula to 'how', when often they are their own secret sauce.

Your willingness is different to your 'how.' When you believe it is possible, when you have the vision, the dissatisfaction, take ownership and are willing to take the first baby step, then you have the opportunity to confront your resistance and move into embracing and being the change you need to see.

Change is inevitable as you evolve your leadership and your business. The question is, are you ready and willing to embrace it and move through the resistance it will cause you to take the next step of action?

## Reflections

This **M=bp2** formula is a simple and effective way to quickly assess your levels of motivation to act. **If you are not moving forward, ask yourself: why?** Getting clear on the root cause of the issue, not the symptom, is the first step to corrective action.

---

1. What is slowing you down?
2. Do you have the belief you can achieve more?
3. What is the goal you have in place that you are emotionally attached to?
4. What is causing you pain and discomfort about staying where you are that could serve as a driver for change?
5. What would you do if you had no fear stopping you?
6. Keep exploring and let your thoughts transcribe on paper. What can you discover about the real reason behind your block and unwillingness to make changes?

# 2

# WHAT LEADER DO YOU NEED TO BECOME?

---

**"Don't bother just to be better than your contemporaries or predecessors, try to be better than yourself."**

— WILLIAM FAULKNER

---

L eadership is at the core of my foundation framework. In the initial stages of business, unless you hire from day one, you will be wearing all the hats and juggling all the balls. Therefore, you are not only the captain of your ship and responsible for its direction, but you are also its only 'employee' too.

I see your CEO role like an eagle. You step out of the doing and regularly visualise, review and plan it from a higher and fresh perspective. This is a different role entirely from the 'in' your business approach where you may fulfil team member activities or be in delivery mode for your clients and customers. Therefore, allocating time to work on the business is critical. I am a big advocate of allocating time in your diary for CEO days, strategy days and as you grow one, team days too. Getting stuck in 'doing' mode won't allow you to strategise and plan forward.

*NOTE: If you are running a business where your priority is generating a small income that meets your needs for a specific period, it will be less important that you think and behave like a CEO. However, if you are looking to grow a business with repeatable, sustainable profit and opportunities to create legacies and assets, it is imperative that you step into a leadership role ahead of having a team.*

You cannot evolve into CEO mode when you are deep in the trenches of the day-to-day operations. You will need to be intentional with your actions, disciplined with your routines and habits and committed to allocating and prioritising time and resources. Spending too much time in team member mode and not allocating time in the diary for CEO activities could risk you becoming the bottleneck to your business growth.

Irrespective of what you call yourself and even if you intend to stay in a 'delivery' capacity for clients, I encourage you to look for ways to make some (if not all) of your role dispensable over time. This means you systematically and strategically let go of the day-to-day, lead and build the strategy which supports growth and hire, develop and inspire a team of whatever size necessary to close the gaps in your business. If you want to achieve certain goals in your business, it won't always be you that has to do it. By hiring, developing and taking a team (of your choosing) on the journey, they can make the vision become a reality with you.

*NOTE: Whilst this book isn't about hiring and building your team, in Question 10 we look at next steps and discuss your first hire if you are just getting started.*

Having worked with a wide variety of businesses and leaders, it goes without saying that every business and leader is different. However, I do believe that there are key stages that most businesses go through as they progress and transition from 'employee to leader'.

## Stage 1 – The boat is bobbing on the water

You are doing it all. The ideas, execution, sales, marketing, delivery to clients, administration, systems, processes and everything in between. It is unlikely you will consider yourself anything other than a business owner at this stage.

Some will stay here indefinitely with no desire to grow. More than half in this stage consider quitting (with a chunk of them seeing this through) because the exhaustion, overwhelm and lack of revenue for their time is too much. It often feels harder than being employed. The non-quitters may get the 'enough is enough' moment and take steps to change. Those who remain decide early on to structure their business ready for growth and quickly embrace their role as leader within this.

## Stage 2 – The sail is set and the boat is moving

You have ascertained your zone of genius and whilst you may still be doing a chunk of the 'doing', you have started to outsource tasks (this could be freelancers or on your payroll). This frees up your time to focus on the income generating activities and other activities that are important for growth.

This is a critical stage. You may feel stuck or overwhelmed as you feel you need more revenue to warrant hiring for the next stage of growth. As you navigate, you will find that the team you have are also wearing many hats too. The challenge with this is that if you start to grow your client base and revenue too quickly without the core team, you run the risk of too high an expectation and failure to deliver to your clients.

It can, if you are not careful, become a reactive place to build from. I advocate hiring in before you feel ready to do so, to prevent scale without infrastructure. There are creative ways to hire your team (or develop an existing one) so you are able to delegate tasks sooner than you think (I will discuss this more in Question 10). It goes without saying that it is important to weigh up the risks involved in making this work out.

## Stage 3 – The speed is up; the boat is cruising

In this stage, you will have a core team in place to provide support. You are embracing your role as a leader and starting to delegate responsibilities and focus in on the CEO behaviours and responsibilities for growth.

The challenge at this stage is team engagement, communication and effective delegation so that they are empowered to make decisions on your behalf and demonstrate equally strong, decisive leadership in your absence.

This is where your systems, processes and policies for hiring, onboarding and development need to continuously be evaluated and reviewed. This will enable you to have a team in place aligned to the values and culture that you want your business to stand for.

A big challenge at this stage is performance and consistency. Often business owners struggle to let go and delegate. Equally, at the opposite end, they over delegate and let go completely – which can, if the team member isn't properly onboarded, result in mistakes and a negative impact on customer service. Therefore, investing in your leadership development is critical as your business grows. This is a wonderful stage when you take the time to reflect, analyse and tweak as you will find that you are able to leverage your time through the skills of others. This means that action happens and you don't have to be involved in it or lead it all.

## Stage 4 – You are sitting at the front of the boat with time

During my time as an operational business partner, I could always tell the strongest leaders in the meeting room. They were chatting with colleagues, relaxed, and still getting incredible results without being present to make it happen in their restaurant or store. When a leader is constantly on the phone, answering and fielding questions from their team, you know you have a problem.

The best leaders let go of their ego and need to control. Instead, they not only encourage and empower their team to make small decisions, they also delegate the things that really do matter that they previously insisted on doing themselves.

In this stage you will not be reviewing and approving everything. Instead, you will have standard operating procedures and processes (SOPS), systems and check ins that enable your team to make decisions on your behalf and find solutions without checking in with you first. You are no longer the leader with team members, you will be the CEO with a group of leaders who are leading and empowering others on your behalf.

You will know you have reached this phase when your team of leaders are:

---

- Creating solutions to existing problems
- Proactively solving problems before they arise
- Highlighting and brainstorming new opportunities and ways to improve
- Thinking for themselves rather than seeking your approval
- Empowering others within their remit to do the same

---

## Stage 5 – You can see the new horizon

When you are 'in' it, it is like working with all the computer tabs open. Overwhelm and 'doing' will not enable you to think creatively and see the next step of the vision and the future opportunities.

Conversely, when you have developed leaders who can think and act on your behalf, refined systems and processes, strong communication in place, a culture of aligned values, and engaged and empowered teams, you will find yourself able to focus again. To see ahead to the next level of your vision. To look at up levelling and imagining what is next.

If you really truly want your business to grow, you will need a vision that is agile and adapts to challenges and opportunities, not the constant motion of bobbing about that 'doing' leaves you in.

A vast number of CEOs spend 25% of their time alone thinking, planning and strategising. You shouldn't be trying to control the day-to-day too much at this stage – how you are performing today is largely down to the work you put into your strategic vision and plan to execute.

In this stage, I would encourage you to be clear on the longer-term vision of what you want from your business. What is your exit strategy? What do you want it to achieve? Where are the challenges? What could cause you to de-rail?

---

You started your business for a reason. Maybe with a dream in mind.

I would put money on the fact that you did not start it because you wanted to work 24/7 'in' the business, getting in your own way and being the bottleneck that stifles growth. Therefore, you need to continually look for ways to free up your time, make yourself dispensable and enable your business to move to and past the original dream you have or had.

As a leader you need to be clear on your destination, map out the journey to get there – but enjoy the journey! Which leads me to our next discussion: your self-awareness and consciousness as a leader.

---

## Reflections

1. Which stage are you at currently?
2. Where do you want your business to be?
3. What is stopping you moving forward right now?
4. What needs to change for you to be leading your business and leveraging your own zone of genius?
5. What could you do differently right now?
6. Who would you value in your team to free up your time?

## How self-aware (conscious) are you?

'The practice of intentionally influencing your thinking, feeling and actions towards your objective(s)'

— BRYANT AND KAZAN

Leadership today requires more of a human element and a rapidness to adapt to change than ever before.

**Lau Tzo was an ancient Chinese philosopher and writer and famously said;**

*"Mastering others is a strength; mastering yourself is power."*

I champion that the best leaders are also great coaches. Self-awareness, curiosity and strong communication skills are some of the greatest skills in a leader's toolkit. Great leaders empower themselves and their teams. These important skills should be kept as sharp as possible to navigate the volume and speed of change that will be thrown your way.

Getting curious about yourself and increasing your self-awareness will not only maximise performance but most importantly help you sense check and align your values, happiness and fulfilment too.

Developing a better sense of yourself is also grounding. It helps you navigate difficult situations with less stress and negative emotion. The more conscious you become of your behaviour, the more intentional your leadership will be. In turn, the greater the ripple and impact on those you work with and support. It also plays a critical role in navigating and embracing change.

### What is self-leadership?

Manz (1986) was the first to define modern self-leadership. He described it as, *"a journey to self-discovery and self-satisfaction, a method of self-influence – a source of controlling your own behaviours and fulfilment."*

In the book, *Self Leadership* Andrew Bryant and Ana Kazan explain that self-leadership is necessary to think effectively, behave congruently and relate empathetically as a leader, and add that all of these qualities make a great human being too. They explain self-leadership as a form of self-monitoring, making you more aware of the consequences of your behaviour.

Self-leadership is the ability to influence yourself to think and behave in a way consistently aligned with who you really are. It is conducive to the pursuit of goals and experiences that are important and relevant to you.

You live in an ever-changing world, full of disruption and change. You must be agile as a leader to navigate. To do this, you must develop your inner game. It is important that as your business grows, you grow yourself as a leader alongside it.

A better understanding of yourself empowers accountability for your behaviour and a move away from blame or finger pointing. It enables greater resilience and ownership and encourages you to reframe your thoughts and beliefs that may be limiting your growth and development. This is key as you grow, because not everything will go your way. Understanding this and watching out for your reactions to situations will speak volumes about how you step up as a leader and develop your awareness and leadership of self.

When you step into a more curious state, with greater awareness and higher levels of self-awareness, you will start to feel more accomplished, independently of what life has handed you. This means you have a greater ability to see the silver lining and opportunity from circumstances outside of your own control. Equally, you will discover more about yourself, what makes you happy, fulfils and motivates you. In this process of discovery, you might discover that what motivates you isn't necessarily grandiose goals or accomplishments. It could be something deeper and more intrinsic.

Greater consciousness can have such a transformational impact on the performance and impact of leaders. If you would like to dig deeper into it and understand some of the differences between consciousness and unconsciousness, I recommend adding *15 Commitments of Conscious Leadership* by Jim Dethmer, Diana Chapman and Kaley Warner Klemp to your library.

These authors provide an example of an unconscious leader and a conscious one (with additional context). They are extreme examples but a useful reference. I have taken the liberty of extracting from their book a summary of these examples by way of comparison.

### *Person A:*

Survives on five hours sleep, has his laptop and phone by his bed and dives in the minute his eyes open to the world. He is committed to some workouts in the week, but never achieves his six a week goal. He rarely has time to spend with his kids even though they give his life meaning. When he is with them, he is rarely fully present as will be multitasking on his phone. His relationship with his wife is functional; they exist as co-parents rather than anything deeper. High levels of adrenaline and copious amounts of caffeine get him through the day and his ethos as a leader and within the culture he has created is one of hustle. No one in his team shares their true feelings, vulnerabilities or speaks candidly with one another. When they do get together, they are indulging in gossip to connect. Person A is regarded as a highly successful leader.

## *Person B:*

Wakes with intention, focuses on allowing time for breathing and meditation. She and her partner invest and make time for each other to connect daily on a deeper level. She has built her business around her family and is always present for breakfast without access to devices. She is collected and taken to work by a driver because she is committed to working in her zone of genius and leveraging her time with support systems and a team to enable her to operate from a place of joy. She has systems that enable her to work smarter and more efficiently. She commits to regular yoga classes and encourages this in her team by making these available in the office. She starts work at 10am. She is focused on her top three priorities for the day and sets aside ninety minutes for her most important work. She understands she does her best mental work in the morning and therefore meetings are scheduled in the afternoon. The team are empowered to make decisions and they all know what constitutes an emergency over a 'drive by interruption'. Strong communication channels are in place that minimize time wasting. The culture is that of openness; vulnerability is encouraged as is ownership of self. They have low turnover and high engagement with low sickness levels. There is lots of fun and playtime available and none of it is an obligation. They have a lifelong learning approach. She checks her email after lunch, not throughout the day. All notifications are off. Boundaries are high and respected throughout. Energy and self-awareness are high. She lives in her zone of genius and empowers everyone around her to do the same. She leaves work at 6.00pm and her work is complete for the day currently. She is in bed for 10.00pm.

She is also a highly successful leader.

## Reflections

1. What insights can you gather from these examples?
2. Are you closer to the version of Person A or Person B?
3. Which version appeals to you more?
4. What might need to change for you to develop your consciousness?

## What strengths could you leverage?

I've always been an advocate of *'do more of what you love.'* Identifying and leveraging your strengths plays to this notion. As we continue together, I will be encouraging you to check that you and any team you go on to hire are on the 'right seat on the right bus.'

It's human nature to respond well to a positive environment and encouragement, rather than the threat of consequence of 'not doing something well.' Positive psychology is aimed at helping people optimise their potential and become happier and more successful at work. It emphasises what is right, rather than what is wrong. It's backed by strong evidence that focusing on strengths and other positive qualities helps us live better, more successful lives at work and outside.

It was my fascination with this subject that led me to become accredited as a Master Strengthscope® Practitioner.

Strengthscope® is the only strengths assessment registered with the British Psychological Society as an accurate measure and predictor of work-based strengths. Its strengths based psychometric profiling enables a whole new level of self-awareness.

**And it matters. Because developing high levels of self-awareness is the first step to moving into high performance.**

It lays the foundation of how emotional and social intelligence is built and helps leaders link their emotions to the effectiveness of their interactions with others.

*Strengthscope® defines strengths as underlying qualities that energise you and you are great at (or have the potential to become great at).*

- **Strengths are natural qualities that energise and excite you the most.** It is these that determine how engaged you are by a task and how you will stick at it.
- **They differ from our competencies.** Whilst our strengths reflect what energises us, competencies are learned skills, knowledge and behaviours we have developed. We are not necessarily energised by our competencies in the same way as our strengths. Competencies alone could see you operating in your zone of excellence and missing the element of joy.
- **Research over the past two decades shows that strengths provide us with the greatest opportunities for development and growth.** They are the areas where we can achieve our highest performance, if we deliberately build skill, knowledge and experience over time.

Another way to look at strengths is to look for clues in your day-to-day and reflective practice about what naturally lights you up or you gravitate towards on the to do list. It is what you love to do (and are naturally energised by) and are already great at or could be something you are passionate about and have the potential to get great at (it is that zone of genius we have been discussing).

Just because you have been an accountant for twenty years and are competent in this field, it won't necessarily mean your energy for it is the same as when you started. You can fall out of love with something and still be good at it (back to the zone of excellence). But you won't perform at your best because you simply don't have the energy to give it your all anymore.

As important as focusing and leveraging strengths are, you must also consider (and not ignore) any potential performance risks too.

There are three main types of performance risk: -

- Your strengths in overdrive
- Any limiting weaknesses
- Other sources of interference - internal and external
  (e.g. perceptions, beliefs, triggers, blind spots, blocks)

Performance risks can be in the background not causing a great deal of challenge for you. If they don't impact your ability to leverage your strengths and lead your business, then there isn't a need to focus on them. I look at performance risks as holes in a boat. Those that sit above the water line need you to simply keep an eye on them. They may cause you problems if the water gets choppy.

It is the performance risks (holes in the boat) beneath the water line that you should give attention to. Ignoring them could result in your boat sinking, irrespective of how incredible the strengths that you are leveraging to keep the boat sailing may be.

The key is to be aware of your performance risks, but not hang your hat on them and give them attention that they really don't warrant.

### How accountable are you for your behaviour?

### When leveraging strengths, I encourage you to develop your attitude and mindset into a solution focused approach.

This is where you will embrace the path of possibility. This means you adopt a growth mindset; embrace challenges and change, take on feedback, persist in the face of setback, find solutions, learn from failure and mistakes and always ask, 'What more can I do?'

Conversely, the path to limitation sees you with a fixed mindset; you avoid challenges, procrastinate on finding solutions, reject feedback, blame others, let setbacks derail you, give up easily, have a heap of limiting beliefs and avoid trying something new.

An analogy I use is *potholes*. Potholes are inevitable on roads, just like obstacles and hurdles are on your business journey. If you can get better at seeing them coming and learn strategies to steer round and ride over them (without them derailing you), you are one part through the battle. Not seeing them ahead may result in your downfall and could slow your journey. It may also cause additional issues for you to address and ultimately take a chunk of time (that you may not have) to climb out. All of this means your journey to higher performance is slower.

## What else will enhance your performance?

To achieve your highest levels of performance, you need to ensure that your strengths add value to the role(s) that you undertake in your business (hence the right seat, right bus reference).

Think of it like building muscle strength. The more you practise using and leveraging your strengths, the more skilled you become in using them across different situations. Your zone of high performance will grow and grow, boosting your results and achievements.

Equally, by leveraging strengths, getting clear on the direction and strategy of your business, alongside developing any gaps in skills, you give yourself the maximum opportunity to achieve your highest level of performance.

By taking these principles and reviewing the same within your team, you give your business the best opportunity to create greater energy, engagement and high performance.

*TIP: This is a brilliant tool when looking at the team you need by your side. As Tony Robbins said, "I don't do anything that I can hire someone else to do better." By bringing in team to do tasks that don't energise you but they love, you are giving your business the greatest opportunity to perform by empowering yourself and your team to all leverage strengths and build that muscle.*

## What is the right way for you to move forward?

Moving from doing it all to leading others who take on the tasks and enable you to operate in your zone of genius won't happen overnight. But if you are keen to grow and scale your business you cannot do it alone.

You will need to become conscious of what strengths you bring to the table and leverage these, whilst gradually hiring others to support you in tasks that leverage their strengths. Essentially, if you hate it or suck at it, aim to hire someone who is energised by it and is a genius (or has the potential to be). Imagine the energy, joy and performance with this approach in your team!

*TIP: It is worth noting at this stage, that the first person you bring in to support you in your team might provide help in your home rather than your business. If you are juggling several roles both personally and professionally, having someone to free up your time from home tasks could enable you to be more productive and achieve higher levels of performance in your work.*

I highlight again that you might also suck at being a CEO. Strategy, vision, direction - it may not be your thing. It may be that you have an incredible product/service that you want to personally deliver to the client, so you actually need to hire in a CEO (or an operator) to help you lead, visualise, strategise and execute. Getting everyone operating in their zone of genius is the key to improving happiness, fulfilment and performance all round.

## Reflections

1. When you think about your strengths and energy consider this:

- What gives you energy?
- What zaps your energy?
- What patterns of behaviour do you notice about yourself?
- What triggers you to move from your path of possibility to one of limitation?
- Get mindful day-to-day. Take the time to tune in to how you are feeling and why. What is this telling you?

2. What activities in your business (or home) are you avoiding or just not getting done that is slowing your progress?

3. What support would game change your business right now?

4. Think about the leader you want to be versus the leader you currently are.

- What impact do you want to have?
- What legacy do you want to leave?

5. If a hot shot leader replaced you tomorrow, where could they be more effective? How would they behave? What actions would they take that you are not right now?

# 3

## WHAT MATTERS MOST TO YOU?

---

**"The real joy in life comes from finding your true purpose and aligning it with what you do every single day."**

— TONY ROBBINS

---

The first step in my foundation framework is finding your purpose. This is one of the most important steps within the framework as it will enable you to grow a business that aligns and is a fit for you first and foremost.

**PLUS, when you hire your team to align with this purpose, they will be more engaged because they believe what you believe. Getting clarity on your purpose helps you:**

- Identify the **WHY** and **HEART** of your business.

- Capture what you **REALLY** want.
- Dictate the **TYPE** of business you want to grow.

When you state your mission in your mission statement you outline the aims (purpose) and values of your business. This statement defines what drives you and reveals your passion as a business. It is the true meaning behind the money you make. When your business lives and breathes its purpose, it will be the same on the outside as it is when you step through the door and go inside. What you see is what you get.

See it as not what you sell, but why you sell it.

Simon Sinek famously talks about starting with WHY. He says, "people don't buy what you do, they buy why you do it. What you do simply proves what you believe." I liken purpose to the fuel in your tank on difficult days. It is the emotional pull that links you to the goals you set yourself. When you know why you are doing something, it gives you more momentum to act. To know your why, you must know more about the layers beneath it - drivers, purpose, happiness. This is what underpins your mission.

---

"We are at our most productive and creative when we are happy and being ourselves at work."

— RICHARD BRANSON

---

Before we dive into your business and what it does and why, I wholeheartedly encourage you to start first and foremost with what matters most to YOU.

In your owner managed business, you are at its core. I urge you to first reflect and act on what you want your life to look and feel like. This is to enable you to design a business that fits the life you choose and fully reflects your mission and values. This will empower you to build a business from a place of joy.

I didn't do this work when I transitioned from employment. I dived headfirst into the doing and whilst I had great brands as clients and some high cash revenue months, I proceeded without intention and said yes to anything and everything that came my way. This is common practice when owner managed businesses start because cashflow is critical. However, over time I found I was moving unintentionally, building a business that wasn't aligned to what mattered most to me. I didn't always leverage my strengths, meaning I often felt like I was walking through treacle. I worked long and unsociable hours and soon the freedom and choice I had left the 9-5 for was a million miles away.

You might think this approach of starting with you is self-indulgent; selfish, even. After all, isn't your business about helping others - supporting your clients, your customers? Don't you need to graft and hustle for success?

Yes, it is all of this (but no thanks to the long-term graft and hustle!). However, as the air hostess says on the plane before takeoff, "Fit the oxygen mask on you first, so that you can then help others." Business takes energy – no matter how ambitious and driven you may be, you cannot continually pour from an empty cup. If you are not working from a place of purpose with space for what matters most to you outside of it, I promise it will feel harder to show up and perform at your best. It won't take long for the cracks to show.

A business without purpose can become unintentional, misaligned, exhausting and overwhelming. It can quickly become no different (and sometimes worse) from the employment you walked away from, but with the added pressure of what goes into making a business successful.

A business that is built from a place of purpose is the first step towards working in complete alignment. This may sound cliché, but when everything aligns and fits, clarity is clearer, energy is higher and you give yourself the best chance to grow your leadership, business model and bottom line.

## What makes you happy?

**Imagine waking each day and knowing that for the most part you are living a life on purpose and leading a business that aligns with this. That doesn't feel like walking through mud, does it?**

I am becoming well known for a few simple tools and methods. I would like to introduce you to one: '**The Happy List**.'

During work with a client, I asked a question I had asked myself in my period of darkness. She was at a crossroad in her business. I pulled out the flip chart and asked her to share everything that made her happy. I explained that it didn't need to be what others value, or what others would want for her, that this was 100% her 'oxygen mask time.' I encouraged her to include moments when she felt her heart swell with joy, when she felt most energised, at her calmest, most content and also the moments she had yet to experience, but if she could, she would thrive. The happy list is a combination of reflections of what has made you feel happy previously and what you truly want to do and achieve into the future to make your heart continue to leap with joy. Another point to note is that it is ever-evolving.

We brainstormed this list. Then I asked her how many of the points she was and wasn't doing. The emotion was immediate. You guessed it; despite a business that was doing well, she wasn't doing enough of what made her happy in it or outside. We went on to explore why and to formulate a strategy to change this so that she could ensure that these foundations of 'happy' were prioritised as part of her own purpose to grow from.

I knew this feeling because when I looked at my own, I too wasn't doing the stuff that lit me up – I had unconsciously drifted further away from the reason I started my business in the first place. It was no wonder I felt so lost and unhappy. I have since asked the same question of hundreds of other leaders in business and continue to check in and ask myself too. My business started to thrive when I focused first on this, because I redesigned my business model to align and built from there.

High performance doesn't come from just one area of work/life. It is a combination of several. Ensuring that you look inwards and keep the scales as balanced as possible will help drive your happiness in the direction that will serve you. Your work, personal and professional development, health, relationships, fun and spiritual practice are just some of the areas to consider. After all, what is the point in driving a super car paid for by work you loathe?

## Where are you heading and why?

When you've discovered what is most important to you, you can then give thought to your business purpose.

Your purpose is ever-evolving because as you and your business develop, so do the goals. By knowing what you are energised by NOW, what you love to do, are most passionate about and how you want your customers to feel enables you to build products and experiences from there.

What about your vision? The place you are heading/creating? I am not talking about the strategic business plan or business goals at this stage; that will come later. I am starting with the overall picture that you see when you close your eyes. What are you looking to create? What does your business look and feel like into the future? What does your life look like? Remember, Van Gogh said, "I dream the painting, then I paint my dream." When you attach to this and know why you are doing what you do, you can get creative with your business model, goals and strategies to help you achieve it (we will chat more about goals in Question 9).

Brands with vision which you may recognise are: -

McDonalds - To be the world's best quick service restaurant experience.

Asos - To be the go-to fashion destination for twenty-some-things, globally.

Disney - Making people happy.

Netflix - Helping content creators around the world to find a global audience.

Every step you take towards your vision supports a tiny step along your purpose path. You can see it clearly in your mind when you close your eyes. Maybe you have it anchored on your phone, on a vision board, on the wallpaper of your PC. The point is you can 100% see it and you sense check your goals and your strategy to feed your desire to reach it every single day.

**If you struggle with finding that vision (many do), start by considering how you want to feel along the journey. What moments are you looking to create? What impact do you want to have? The more you explore this and peel the onion, insights and aspirations will start to unravel.**

**But if the longer-term vision feels too hard and too far off, think ahead to twelve months from now. What do you see? How do you want to feel? What would you love to achieve? Start small: you can look further at a later stage.**

---

### Reflections

Regarding your business purpose, what impact do you want to have on the lives of others?

1. How do you want them to feel?
2. What is it you want them to experience when they encounter you/your team/products?

As part of this purposeful work, I recommend you take the time to dig deeper into your vision too and ensure that this feels in alignment to your purpose.

- What do you want the future to look like?
- What is it that is compelling to you about it?
- Is it heartfelt and do you feel deeply connected to it?

---

## What do you value most?

"Values are a set of words and sentences/paragraphs that state or suggest behaviours that your company have decided are valuable, unique and important." (*Bringing your Values out to Play – Debra Corey*)

Values define who you are, what you stand for, what you believe in and how you will behave. They should serve as guidelines and guideposts for you and for those who work with you.

Values are the principles or standards of behaviour; one's judgement of what is most important.

Values should run through the veins of your business and should be an integral part of your hiring strategy too. Walking and talking your values authentically as the CEO of your business is critical. Remember that everything you do and say will likely be duplicated by those around you.

When you are working in a way that aligns and lives out with your purpose and your values, it really helps things flow. You gain alignment with the right clients, the team that you hire and the principles of how you work day-to-day.

Finding these values, passion, energy and the stuff that truly fuels your fire is vitally important for you and your business.

Values are only important if you know them, demonstrate them, hire to them and communicate them to your team. They shape your culture and become the lifeblood of your business, not just statements stuck on a wall.

---

"Values are needed as principles that guide our behaviour while we're scaling the mountain we set to climb."

— KEN BLANCHARD AND GARRY RIDGE
(FROM *BRINGING YOUR VALUES OUT TO PLAY*)

---

In Built to Last: Successful Habits of Visionary Companies, Jim Collins and Jerry Porras say that you do not create or set values from scratch; instead, you discover them. By reflecting on what you currently say, do, believe, want and feel passionate about, you will discover what your values really are.

You can start to see why alignment across the areas I outlined is so important. By discovering your values, you start to discover your purpose and vice versa. The values that you discover will also help and support you to achieve the mission that you set yourself as part of your purpose.

Much like your happy list, when you live, breathe and lead your values, you will feel so much better for it. You will perform better, show up better, lead better and recognise others for it too.

In your quest to get your business growing, you might question why this is important or indeed if it is a priority right now. Equally, if you are running the operation alone, who else needs to know so early on?

Don't wait on this important piece of work. It is important. Without discovering your values, you run the risk of building a business and brand that draws the wrong clients to you, attracts the wrong team support, sees you hanging out with the wrong colleagues and potentially having in place products that don't align.

A potential client needs to be able to trust you, your business and brand. If you talk about one thing and behave in a totally different way, they are unlikely to trust you and this could risk your reputation or growth moving forward.

Remember, I didn't do this work when I started. As a result, I didn't always work with others that aligned with my values. It meant that at times I found myself taking on clients who behaved in ways that went against what I believed in.

----

### Reflections

Some questions to ask when reflecting and discovering your values are: -

1. What is most important to you?
2. What makes you different from your competitors?
3. What is a non-negotiable for you?
4. What energises you?
5. What drains you?

6. What rattles your cage and makes you frustrated or compromised?
7. What behaviours are important to you that you want to see throughout your business from others?
8. What promises do you make to others in terms of your behaviour?
9. What behaviours are important in order for you to fulfil your purpose and your mission?

---

## What boundaries do you have in place?

*Boundary — a line which marks the limits of an area; a dividing line.*

I promise my clients that I will get them working in a way that is right for them. For the most part, this means more TIME to do things that matter most outside of work.

This leads me perfectly to one of my most popular tools - the Personal Contract™.

When I talk about personal contracts, I am talking about your business boundaries.

In your former life as an employee, it is highly probable you will have had a contract of employment with your employer. It would have helped you understand what was expected of you and the boundaries you had to work within for your role.

However, when starting a business, most won't give this a great deal of thought.

As a result, the boundary lines you create can become blurred.

All relationships, whether personal or professional, need boundaries. They mark a territory and makes clear what is acceptable, what isn't and sets out what you will and won't accept.

Your boundaries also tell others how you will allow them to treat you. Without boundaries, people may take advantage of you because you haven't set limits about how you expect to be treated.

Boundaries in business include who you will and won't work with as well as what is acceptable to you regarding how you work and this is where the personal contract comes into play.

Another reason I love the personal contract is that it makes you very intentional about how you will work – by setting a commitment and boundary for yourself.

### So, what do I mean by your Personal Contract™?

Well, they are your version of a contract of employment, but for you.

It is a contract that aligns with your purpose and values and is communicated with your clients (and team) to help establish a deeper sense of trust and connection. The other benefits of a personal contract and greater boundaries include: -

- Clear priorities (I call this your default setting), resulting in you not feeling guilty about saying no if out of alignment.
- Empowerment to make informed decisions about who you will work with and how you will work with them.
- Better control of what you do day-to-day, week-to-week, both in business and in your life. Better habits and success routines.
- The freedom and choice to do more of what you love and less of what you don't. This is the permission to

operate from your zone of genius – including the precious gift of time off! This can also support your team hiring strategy too.

- Stronger relationships with your team and clients because you are clear about your boundaries and availability. This will deepen the trust between you.
- Greater consciousness about how you work at your best. There is more joy and less resentment, so you enjoy the journey. You create a way of working that enables you to bring your best self forward. You live out your values. You commit to doing only what is right for you. It also is a great starting point to look deeper into your zone of genius and the team you need with you to enable you to do this.

**What do you include in your Personal Contract™?**

It is less about what you write down and more about your intentions and commitment to yourself. It is your contract, so you can include whatever feels most important to you. To get you started, here are some recommendations: -

- Your specific zone of genius – what you love to do
- The outline of your main role and focus areas
- The hours you will work
- The days you will work and what you will do on those days
- When you will take off time for holidays
- Where you are going to work. What is the right environment for you?
- What your success routine is and daily/weekly/monthly habits. How will you perform the tasks of your role and key responsibilities? For

example: checking email at 10am and 3pm only.
Meetings on a Tuesday and Wednesday morning.
Creative work on a Thursday. One CEO Day a month
to work on the business to review progress against
KPIs and Goals. Strategy days with team quarterly.

- Your financial target for the year and what this equates
to in value for an hour of your time. This is useful so
you don't compromise on your pricing strategies.

I have outlined some additional options to consider when
thinking about these boundaries with your ideal clients.

1. Be sure to communicate your availability. If you plan
to have days covered by someone in your team when
you are not available, be sure to communicate this to
your team and clients, so they know who they will be
liaising with day-to-day.

2. Be clear on when and how clients can contact you.
What is included in the scope of your work for the
client and what falls outside of scope and what will
happen in this situation (e.g. extra fees to be charged).
Get a contract and/or agreement sent out prior to you
working together. Prepare for the worst to happen in
your relationship, even though you expect the best.

3. Set up consequence if agreements or contracts are
breached. As wonderful as most clients are, there will
be times when it doesn't work out. What will happen if
a client doesn't turn up for a call with you or pay their
invoice on time? Establish ahead of time how you will
deal with these worst-case scenarios so that you are
prepared ahead of the event. Then you can just follow
the process consistently when you need to.

4. Be sure to share and communicate these expectations

clearly to clients so there isn't any grey area (as per agreements/contracts as outlined in step 3). Keep records of your agreements for reference and be mindful of the most appropriate way to communicate with clients. We will go deeper on the customer journey in Question 4 but consider each touch point in turn and make sure that there are not any confusing sign-posts that could cause you issues further down the line and compromise boundaries.

5. Stick to these boundaries. Be committed to your default contract (note, it is ok to tweak this and sometimes work outside of it if you need to, but this is the exception rather than the rule. Be courageous and step away from a request from a client or a potential client if it doesn't align with your boundaries. If someone isn't right for you, could they be a mutually better fit for someone else in your network that you could connect them with? You can say no and still be kind and respectful, please remember that.

As your business structure evolves and you look at the team you need to support your growth, you could consider hiring someone to take the lead for your customer experience. This is all down to what you want your business to look and feel like and where you see your own zone of genius playing out best within the business you are creating and scaling.

It's your business and you get to decide how you run it. By deciding what's important and communicating your business boundaries to clients and holding yourself accountable to them, you set up the roadmap for success - for you and for your clients.

In summary...

Your vision is your mountain peak. Your goals are the stepping-stones on the journey to getting there. Your values are the commitments to behaviour that are most important to you and this will dictate how you show up, who you take with you and the way in which you communicate both internally and externally. The personal contract is your set of boundaries and the agreement with yourself in living out and protecting two important areas – time and joy.

---

### Reflections

1. What would you include in your personal contract?
2. Do you have opportunities to improve your boundaries?
3. Who/what is pushing your boundaries right now?
4. What could change moving forward to improve how you feel about boundaries?

---

**Personal contracting is an integral part of the work I do with my clients. Therefore, I have created a separate guide to help you dive deeper into yours. Just scan the QR code to get access.**

# WHO DO YOU WANT TO WORK WITH?

---

**"Be sure you positively identify your target before you pull the trigger."**

— TOM FLYNN

---

W ithin the Purpose step of the framework, I include the important topic of your ideal client.

**So why is it important to know?**

You cannot sell your products to everyone. Irrespective of what you offer or how brilliant it is, it will not be suitable for everyone.

*There is a saying 'sell to everyone, sell to no-one.'*

To sell more products or services, you need to target the right client who needs and wants what you are selling and trusts that you are the right person or company to help. If you want to grow your pipeline of prospects, you need to position your marketing message to the right person.

Getting clarity and having an Ideal Client Avatar (ICA) will make you more able to communicate powerfully with the people who are most likely to become your clients and customers.

*Note: A Client Avatar is a marketing term also called an Ideal Client Profile or a Buyer Persona. An Avatar is simply a fictional character you refer to when considering your communications and messaging.*

Not everyone is right for you. You want to be like Marmite. Resonate your message with some, but not all.

Your marketing, messaging and positioning (market positioning refers to the ability to influence consumer perception) should talk to one person – your Ideal Client.

By knowing who your ideal client is, you can then get curious about them. Ask, listen and learn more about their specific behaviour, problems and purchasing habits. You can then respond and map out your entire business to support them. Having deep knowledge of your ideal client helps you narrow the scope of your marketing and tailor your products to offer a solution to their needs.

When you understand your target client, you can tailor your marketing and messaging to reach them more effectively. When you do this, they will see you, hear you and feel like you are speaking directly to them.

However... these people also need to exist and need or want what you are selling!

## Who don't you want?

**Let's start back to front.**

**To find out who you want to help, let's start with who you don't.**

**Why?** Because bad clients will STEAL your SOUL. I'll bet that some of your boundaries being pushed right now are down to you working with a less than ideal client.

The beauty of running your own show is you get to choose who you want to hang out with. Why then would you want to draw people to you that are not aligned to your values? Why would you draw those to you who want you to work at times of the day that don't suit you?

I wonder, do any of the following scenarios sound familiar?

- You feel pulled in a million different directions and overwhelmed with everything on your list.
- Your clients constantly ping you outside of work hours or request work above and beyond your capacity.
- You spend so much time fielding client requests that you don't have time to work on your priority projects.
- You say yes to requests and invitations because it feels easier than to say no.
- You feel increasingly resentful of others' demands on your time.
- You feel run ragged, tired, and exhausted and never have any time for yourself.

If you answered yes to any of these statements, it's safe to say there are some clients who are pushing your boundaries.

## Reflections

This is important - before you dive into who you want to attract, let's start by getting clear on those you don't.

1. Who have you worked with in the past who has been difficult?
2. Who hasn't appreciated your value?
3. Who drains your energy? (Consider the calls/emails you dread.)
4. Who complains about your pricing?
5. Who has pushed your boundaries?
6. Who has expected you to work over and above their contract/agreement?
7. Who do you just not feel aligned with?

## Who is your dreamy client?

You now know that the more you understand, live and breathe your ideal client, the greater impact your marketing, sales, content, communication, branding and overall message will have in reaching them. Anything and everything you do to attract customers should always refer to your ICA Profile.

The important thing to remember is when you pull together your brand positioning, messaging and offers, talk and provide a solution to this dreamy client only. Talk to just one person.

It can be helpful to give them a name and a fictional photo so you can really dive into them and their world. I like to create an overview on A4 and keep it visible so I can consider them in my marketing and messaging.

You start with describing them.

What does a day in their life look like? What is their background, their professional status, financial situation? How do they behave on and offline? What keeps them awake at night? What are their hopes and aspirations? What makes them laugh? What are they passionate about? What do they feel strongly about? What is important to them? How could you help? What do they want or need from you?

The more you understand, the better you can communicate with them.

You can then validate your assumptions by speaking with your current and dreamy clients and getting their feedback and insight (you could do this through surveys, 1:1 discussions, focus groups). Then you will need to go into the characteristics and feelings/emotions. It is critical to always seek to understand them. Never stop doing this. The more you listen and learn, the more you can respond and provide what they need as your business evolves.

## Reflections

1. Why does your product/service matter to them?
2. Who do you enjoy working with?
3. Think about your values/your personal contract – what is non-negotiable?
4. Who needs what you do the most?
5. Who has been your favourite client to date?

6. What brings your ICA joy?
7. What keep them awake at night?
8. What challenges do they face?
9. What aspirations do they have?
10. What do they value?
11. Where do they hang out?
12. What questions do they ask?

I encourage you to get creative with this. A visual representation of your dreamy client is a great way to remind you of them in your messaging to them.

---

## What experience do you want your customer to have?

I am a firm believer that your unhappiest customers are your greatest source of opportunity to improve. However, the aim is to proactively get the feedback before your customer becomes unhappy.

Once you have figured out who you want to attract, it is as important to think about the journey your customer will go through to work with you and the experience you want to provide.

The customer journey is every touch point and sum of experiences that customers go through when interacting with you and your business. Instead of looking at just a part of the process or experience, the customer journey documents every step and the full experience of being a customer with you.

Your customer's journey begins at the point of awareness and moves them through to them becoming advocates of your business and brand. As shown in the diagram below, you can see the vast number of touch points you must consider when you are reviewing their experience with you (this is not an exhaustive list).

The easier you make it for them at each touch point, the more likely they are to action and move to the next step with you.

For example, how easy it is to navigate your website? Find you on social media? Contact you? How easy it is to book or buy from you? To get advice? Provide a review? How easy is it to access your products or services? Things move at an alarming pace and our attention spans are shorter than ever. You must make it easy to navigate and make a buying decision and provide incredible after service once they have had the product or service from you too.

Put yourself in the shoes of your customer. Experience the journey through their eyes, test out your product or service. If you cannot do this, then it becomes even more important to set up processes/systems to enable you to gain feedback along the way, so you can quickly respond and change to meet evolving needs.

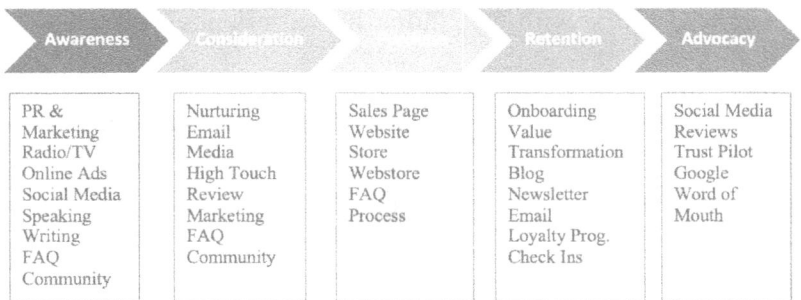

| Awareness | Consideration | | Retention | Advocacy |
|---|---|---|---|---|
| PR & Marketing Radio/TV Online Ads Social Media Speaking Writing FAQ Community | Nurturing Email Media High Touch Review Marketing FAQ Community | Sales Page Website Store Webstore FAQ Process | Onboarding Value Transformation Blog Newsletter Email Loyalty Prog. Check Ins | Social Media Reviews Trust Pilot Google Word of Mouth |

## Reflections

1. What are the customer touch points for each of your products/services?
2. How do you get feedback from them?
3. How easy is it to buy from you?
4. What feelings do you want to evoke in them?
5. How can you make them feel special?
6. What do they see when they search for you on the internet?
7. How well do you position yourself to them?
8. What will they remember about you, irrespective of whether they decide to work with you?
9. Where and when are you losing them?
10. How could you automate some of the steps?
11. What opportunities are there to improve?
12. Who is responsible for your customer service?

These questions are to guide your reflection so you can assess how you are currently performing and how you can improve your customer's experience at every single touch point. WOW them. Add VALUE. Increase LOYALTY and EASE. Create an army of FANS.

# 5

# WHAT PRODUCTS ARE YOU SELLING?

---

**"Don't find customers for your products,: find products for your customers."**

— SETH GODWIN

---

Successful business growth depends on a scalable business model that will increase profits over time, by growing revenue while avoiding cost increase.

Step 2 of my framework focuses on your products and business model.

There is no single definition of a business model. The concept started simple – how will your business make its money? Today, it considers customers, goals and strategy. I simply ask, how will your business operate? Your business model should identify sources of revenue by getting clear on the products that it will be making available to your ideal client.

The attribute of a good model is that it aligns with your vision, values, purpose and personal contract and of course that the products and services meet the needs/desires of your dreamy clients and customers. It should be both robust and agile, evolving to meet the fast-paced changing needs and landscape around you.

For clarity, a product offering is either tangible (a physical product or object such as a candle or car) or intangible (such as a course, insurance or consultancy services).

A product mix is an offer of more than one product or service that relates to your core product offering. I am a big advocate of a mix of offers to diversify the risk that one product you offer could become obsolete.

As an example, when I started my business, my focus (although not niche) was on HR consultancy services. Having one client on a retainer that paid me enough to cover my base line operating expenses and salary felt like a great alternative to employment. However, this approach meant I was putting all my eggs in one basket. The risk to me was high. If this one retained client pulled from the contract, my income would disappear. Also, this was not me leading a business, this was effectively me contracting. I had gone from being on someone's payroll as an employee to charging more and working freelance as an HR Consultant. It was equivalent to being employed. It paid more but had no additional benefits.

There is a difference between offering contracting services (which is what I was doing) and leading a business with a mix of products to an ideal client. Neither is right or wrong, but you need to understand which is a better fit and lower risk for you. My advice would be, look to diversify your risk with multiple income streams and/or have accessible finances to cover should you find yourself without cashflow. This could be money put aside or insurance.

*TIP: If more than 30% of your revenue comes from one client in your business, I recommend you review your risk and opportunity to diversify/cover cashflow.*

A good product mix will consist of width, depth and consistency:

**Depth** is considering how many different types of core customer you can satisfy. Within my business model, my product mix allows me to focus on my core customer but provide alternative products to them at different stages of their journey (depending on their budget and how much access to me they want). It isn't intended to be a linear model; my customers can jump in at any level and go up/down or depart as they need.

As an example, take a car company. They have an economy car, sports car and luxury; meaning they meet the needs of different types of customers. This differs from a car company who specialise only in luxury models.

**Width** is the product line within your core offering. For example, you specialise in coffee. But you offer cakes, biscuits, china, cutlery, books and tea alongside. This means you may be less susceptible to fluctuations at different times for your products (due to seasonal impact or supply chain) and therefore diversify your risk.

**Consistency** relates to the connection between the products in your mix and how they reach your customer. This also makes it easier to perform suggestive selling and recommend closely linked products. I recommend when you start in business to get one vertical line in your mix stable before diversifying. I say this because if you start another vertical which is unrelated to your core product you run the risk of having several unrelatable products that overwhelm you and confuse your audience. As someone once said to me, you cannot ride two horses with one ass! When you are more established (with team support in place), then another vertical line that further diversifies your risk and brings in more revenue could be more viable.

I always refer to Gordon Ramsey in US Kitchen Nightmares when I work with my clients on their business model and product mix. Every time he goes into an underperforming restaurant, he discusses the menu. The restaurants that struggle often have an overcomplicated, lengthy list of options available. He always streamlines it. He gets them to focus on fewer options and get this right consistently before anything else.

The same applies in your business model. Focus on the one ideal client you want to help and support, listen to what they tell you they want or need and keep your product offering simple in response. You can evolve the offering as you go. Get one thing right, then move on to developing the next and so on.

Before we discuss this further, let me clarify some revenue options available:

## Recurring Revenue

I am a huge advocate of creating recurring revenue in your business model. This at a minimum helps you to predictably cover your base line operating expenses.

Recurring revenue is simply a portion of a company's revenue that is expected to continue in the future. It helps create stability as it can be counted on at regular intervals.

If I can encourage you to have one goal, look at how you can make your business revenue as predictable as possible and where possible cover your base line operating expenses. This strategy helps you get away from the feast and famine roller coaster trap that most owner managed businesses find themselves in. Some clients will initially tell me that their product offering makes this impossible, but when we discuss and look at options creatively, they are surprised at what they can do.

## Passive Revenue

I was first introduced to the concept of passive revenue when I set up my network marketing company in partnership with an umbrella organisation.

It is the generation of revenue after most of the work is done. For example, royalties from books, movies, property, investment or an evergreen online course/product.

Most of us are not singers or actors and cannot count on the radio or TV simply filling up our bank account because our song or film has been played. Let me be clear - passive isn't about you not doing any work. You do most of the work upfront and put some additional effort in along the way to earn the income. You can also create semi-passive products where you still do some work, but it is minimal (and more people shouldn't mean more work), therefore it gives you scope to reach more people without increasing overheads/time. A membership model and live group development programme are two examples of this.

Other examples include, but are not limited to, stocks, business or other investments, property, books and courses.

## Time Leveraging

This is another important consideration. Small businesses often stay solo or small because of concerns about hiring. This is most apparent in the UK, probably due to employment legislation. By taking this approach, it means the owner of the business limits their growth (and increases their workload and overwhelm) because time is limited to the 24 hours available to one person in one day.

Time leveraging is looking at ways to create more time.

It could be through hiring in team on your payroll to take over tasks not in your zone of genius – freeing up your time to be the CEO lead and/or business developer or focus on delivering to clients. You may decide that your first team member will perform administrative tasks or that they will take on a revenue generating role like sales or business development.

It could also be a model whereby you license your product, service or brand. Others can deliver it through their own business and make you a royalty payment to do so. This means more ideal clients can be reached without reliance on you and could also create additional passive revenue streams.

It could be an agency type model whereby you take the role of CEO and business developer/strategist and hire in a team to provide the delivery service (either on payroll/freelance). This means you reach more clients, create more revenue. (Note, your costs will increase with this approach, so watch out for your profit margins – we discuss this more in Question 8.)

Or you might be interested in a reaching many model. This is the semi-passive option. You create a product or service and deliver it to larger numbers, rather than to one at a time. This can be done through large events, workshops, online courses, group programmes, memberships, subscriptions – the list goes on. I first introduced this into my model when I started a small group in-person mentoring programme which was a mastermind. It enabled me to go from helping one person at a time to helping more using the same amount of time.

The key to this is to make time to think creatively about what options are best for you now and for the future of your business.

## What is an Asset?

Whilst discussing the various options for your product mix, it important to talk about assets.

An asset is an item of property owned by a person or company that is regarded as having value. It can meet its debts and commitments or legacies.

Types of assets can include dividends, bonds, investing in another business, lending money to another business, real estate (renting/investing/vacation), affiliate marketing, domain purchasing, online courses, digital products, video ads (you tube), stock photos, books, ebooks, audio books, licensed music or training and so much more.

These products or services only become an asset when you have broken even and paid off your debt. Therefore, it is a generator of cash - or could be. For example, your house, if it has a mortgage, is not an asset; it is a liability until paid off in full.

This is important to understand because depending on the vision you have for your business, you may want to consider creating assets that you can sell in the future as part of your exit strategy from the business.

## Reflection

### What do you want from your business?

- Is it to provide enough revenue to pay yourself, cover bills and provide a certain standard of living that you exit at any time you decide (still ensure you have considered your retirement plans)?
- Do you want your business to provide revenue to invest elsewhere that creates a further revenue stream and potential asset?
- Or do you want to invest time and capital into your business so that you are able to sell it as an asset as part of your exit strategy?

## Your Business Model

Whatever you choose, your business model and mix of products need to align with what we have discussed so far. It should aim to leverage your strengths and enable you to create the flow of cash needed to provide the life and vision you have. It should align to what and how you want to work. If in time you want to work your business part time, make sure your business model will enable you to do this. The numbers need to add up.

## Value Ladder

A value ladder is a useful and visual way to look at your products/services in ascending order of value and price. The notion is, as clients ascend the ladder, the value increases as does the cost.

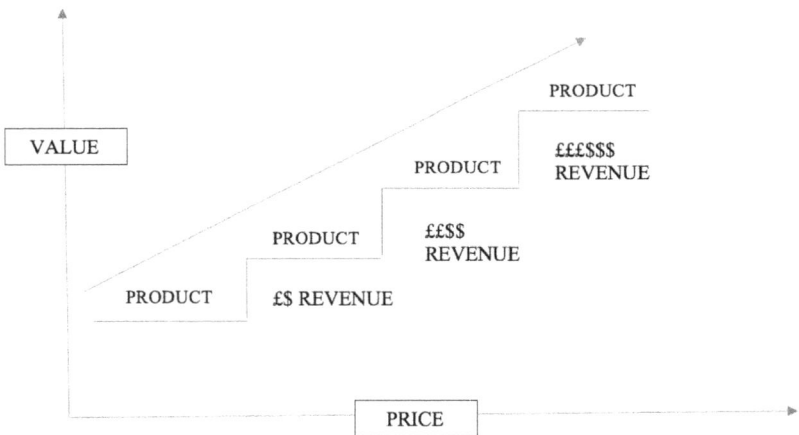

It also helps you see where your opportunities for up and down sells may be. This can also be referenced when you look at your sales funnel, which we will discuss in Question 6.

Not everyone you talk to will move through the ladder. Some may come straight in at your premium product and move to an alternative cheaper option thereafter. The aim is that you continue to offer and provide solutions to your existing clients to encourage them to stay with you. New client acquisition is costly in time and money and therefore it is a great strategy to have additional products available to retain existing clients and customers.

By having only one product without width/depth in your mix, it is highly probable you are leaving money on the table. By asking, listening and responding to your client needs, you can maximise the value you offer, the length of time you retain them and the opportunities you create for additional sales, alongside new ones.

**Example: -**

Let's imagine you offer only one product at £500 and have four people interested in buying it.

- Two of those you offer the £500 product, buy it. However, one is keen on your support but only has a £250 budget. It isn't that they don't value your offering, they genuinely only have this budget to spend.
- If you only have one product and don't look at how you could further support this client with a lower priced product (assuming you want to work with them) you could lose £250 in a sale.
- Likewise, the fourth potential client is looking for more. They would like to work with you and have £1000 to invest in you. They don't want your £500 option.
- In only having one product, you have potentially not

provided value and service to clients three and four and left £1250 on the table.

I am not saying that you should cater for EVERY potential client. I want you to say NO to clients who are not right for you. However, the reason I have the mix of depth in my business model and product mix is for this exact reason.

If someone approaches me for support and doesn't have the budget for my mastermind or group programme, I have the option of my private members area - The Business Leaders' Lounge. If I get enough queries from clients I want to support and I don't have the value on offer that they are looking for, I look to evolve my mix and create it.

I will always sense check that these are my ideal clients. Equally, I only deliver products that leverage my zone of genius and bring me joy in my work. I encourage you to do the same. I also like to keep things simple (think back to Gordon Ramsey and his menu).

You are not looking to please everyone, but you do need to take into consideration that your potential customers might want different options within what you offer.

Another point to note is that sometimes people want to try before they fully invest in your premium product. What do you offer at a lower price that could enable them to dip their toe in first and check your products (and your business) are right for them? This approach can help you with retention of clients too.

***TIP: Low cost 'try' options could be a free PDF, ebook or low-cost taster offer, pack of cards, shorter taster treatment or session, short training or a power hour.***

Looking at your value ladder and model could not only improve the service and value you offer but could also have a positive impact on your cashflow in the process.

Please ensure when you create your products and pricing that you focus on value to your client. It isn't just about the price being right for you (and charging your worth), it is the value that they perceive your product to provide and how well you meet this in your delivery (not forgetting the overall experience you provide throughout their journey with you). We will discuss how you acquire clients in Question 6, as well as how you position your messaging to your ideal client.

---

### Reflection

This is your business. YOU get to decide its model, your mix of products and revenue streams. You also get to decide how you want to lead it and be in the trenches. How involved will you be in its delivery and services versus your role as CEO?

1. What insights do you have about your current product mix and offering? Are they right? Do you enjoy delivering them? Do your clients get value? What are your clients asking for more of?
2. When you consider your value ladder, where might be your current gaps? What products could you add/remove?
3. How well is your current business model serving you?
4. What else do you think needs to change?
5. What ways could you leverage your time?
6. Do you want to always be involved in delivering the

service/product or would you rather hire a team to do this?

7. How big are your financial aspirations?
8. What ideas do you have to scale your offering?
9. How do you prefer to work? 1:1 / groups / on or offline or is this not applicable? What other ways of delivery are relevant to your business?
10. How much freedom do you want?
11. How many of your products do you need to sell in order to meet your financial goals? (More on this in Question 7.)

# 6

## HOW WILL YOU GET CLIENTS?

---

**"People don't want a quarter-inch drill – they want a quarter-inch hole."**

— THEODORE LEVITT

---

The next step in my framework is positioning. This is how you position your business, brand and product offerings to those you want to work with. Positioning is essentially the way your customers perceive what it is you offer them and is integral when you are considering how you will acquire new customers and clients.

You know by now that you wear many hats leading a business (unless you hire a team). Two of the most important activities to prioritise daily are your marketing and sales, because without sales, you do not have a business.

I will make a disclaimer - I do not claim to be a sales or

marketing expert. I am a work in progress and currently hiring into these roles within my own business.

However, I have first-hand experience that means my business has grown with me as the lead in both marketing and sales to date. I have learnt from some fantastic sales and marketing specialists and am fortunate to continue tapping into this support and knowledge for the benefit of my business and clients. To respond to the question of how to get clients, I will dive into my toolbox of acquired knowledge to share with you.

This question is a big one. In fact, it is so vast that it deserves its own book and is one of the most common questions my clients ask. It is why I bring in several marketing and sales experts to support my clients in my Get Set for Success™ LIVE programme. For extra support in this area, I strongly recommend you look at the reference section of this book, where I suggest suitable books and experts who are best placed to support you further.

## How do you grow your audience?

Before we dive into your marketing and sales functions, let's briefly discuss the importance of building your audience.

In the old days before the mass growth of the internet, a company would find a gap in the market, fill with a product, determine a price and sell to the customer.

Customers have way more insight and control these days. They have the power to truly love on brands: to get into their world and become a part of their tribe of followers. As a result, a brand has an opportunity to create loyal fans who will go wherever it goes. These fans get stuck in, promote the brand to their friends and enable it to reach and network on a mass scale.

But this type of loyalty and following takes strategy, time, consistency and a whole heap of graft (either by you or as someone you hire in to lead your marketing efforts). To get this in your world, you must build the audience first and position what you are offering in a way that resonates with them and makes them want to go one step further to buying from you.

Without an audience that will buy from you, you risk having an expensive product that gets dusty on the shelf.

Daniel Priestley in his brilliant book, *Oversubscribed*, says:

---

*"There are restaurants that people line up for, products that you have to pre-order months in advance and tickets that sell out the day they are released."*

*"These are the brands that don't chase clients — clients chase them."*

*"A product or a brand reaches a level of being oversubscribed when there are more buyers than sellers. When demand massively outstrips supply."*

---

It is your audience who get to decide if you have a brand. They decide if what you are offering is of value to them. If you don't have a brand, you have just an idea.

An analogy I like to use when I think of building my audience is the concept of filling empty theatre seats.

Imagine a theatre of empty red chairs; your role (or someone in your company) is to position your brand and products and create attention, interest and awareness to fill these chairs with your ideal clients. These are the people who value your brand

and at some point, may consider buying from you. In a sales funnel, this would be at the top.

They will want to get to know your business, follow your story, have their questions answered, get updates, insights and inspiration and be keen to hear testimonials from your existing clients. This is where your content marketing is key. Let them get to know you and give them what they want and need to move one step further forward to buying from you. It is important to point out that your audience will likely be a mix of potential buyers, supporters, brand ambassadors and those who will influence others who need or want your product.

Through your marketing and messaging, those in the red chairs who resonate with your messaging will start to get up and head towards you on the stage with questions that need answering. They will want to make sure that what you offer is going to fit what they need or think they want at that time. They may talk to each other and share experiences and reviews. This is the next step in your sales funnel.

You need to be prepared for these questions. You would also be wise to answer these questions ahead of time, enabling you to speed up the decision-making process. This is where your content, free offers and low-cost products (and any other assets) can be helpful as they help answer the questions, demonstrate your credibility and showcase your expertise and value.

Some who come to the stage will become your customers. Others may go back to their seat as the timing isn't right and will need longer to consider you. Others may opt out and leave.

Your job is to keep the red chairs full through effective positioning within your marketing (this becomes your pipeline) and keep a continual drip coming through to the next stage and beyond thanks to your sales and marketing activities collectively.

Your products and content therefore need to match what those in the red chairs are telling you they need. What you don't want to do is position yourself, draw in their attention and then be unable to meet their expectations with your products. Do not over promise and under deliver!

Therefore, your product mix and business model need to be robust and agile equally to meet their evolving needs.

Don't assume. Seek to continually understand. Ask, listen, learn and respond.

## How important are Marketing and Sales?

It is fair to say that Marketing and Sales (unless you have a prior career in them) are often two of the greatest hurdles you will need to overcome and develop skills in to build your business (hence the multitude of questions my clients ask me).

But and I cannot emphasise this enough, **you cannot ignore them**. You must decide as the leader of your business to either upskill, invest time and take responsibility to action or invest money and hire others to execute for you. I repeat. **You cannot ignore them!**

If you are going to position your business in the right way to the right potential clients and customers, it is important to firstly understand and appreciate the difference between marketing and sales. They are separate interventions that support the growth of your business. They do this individually and collectively: they need a unified approach.

## Marketing

There are several definitions of marketing on the web.

The one I like is from Peter Drucker, an Austrian Management Consultant.

*'The aim of marketing is to know and understand the customer so well that the product or service fits him/her and sells itself – ideally marketing should result in a customer who is ready to buy.'*

At a fundamental level in your marketing, you want to understand your customers and work hard at building and maintaining great relationships with them. Brands who do this well will find that their audience follows them wherever they go. Provided that they are living and breathing the values and ethos that they talk about, they maintain both trust and loyalty along the journey.

Marketing is about the deep psychological understanding of customer needs. Every innovation in history will show you that a true understanding of a human's need combined with the vision to deliver is key to its success.

Marketing isn't an overnight story to success. There are no quick wins. It takes time to build trust and to develop your position in the marketplace with your ideal client.

There are several types of marketing – digital and offline. You need to decide and determine which marketing type(s) are the right fit for you and your business. Please don't feel like you must do what everyone else is doing or that one type fits all.

I like to think of marketing (and sales) as a conversation between two people. We don't know each other all that well, but great conversations will lead you to understand your ideal client's needs better. When you understand their needs, you can better position your offering and provide solutions and products that meet their needs and provide an incredible experience along the way.

Phil M Jones is an absolute legend in the art of great conversation. I have had the good fortune to spend time in his company over the years and cannot find anyone better than him to help you in this area. His book *Exactly What to Say* has pride of place in my library and is always gifted to my private and group clients when we start working together.

He endorses my advocacy that curiosity is a gift in our toolkits as leaders. Phil champions that we create opportunities by first asking the question.

If we don't seek to understand our potential clients, how can we build a relationship and in turn create an opportunity for our products or services to be the solution that they have been seeking?

This simple practice is gold. Whether you are at the bar talking to a stranger, at a networking event or on an online social platform, interested really is interesting. If you take the time to seek a better understanding through questions, it provides you with an opportunity to not only build a better relationship, but also to best respond to what they are telling you they most need.

Another great book that I refer to and recommend to my clients is Marcus Sheridan's *They Ask, You Answer*. He discusses the simplicity of creating a profitable inbound marketing strategy based on quality content. The clue is in the title. It is all about the questions; how you ask, listen and respond. This book highlighted to me that content marketing is simply the art of telling valuable stories and responding in your content to your potential customer's questions proactively at every opportunity.

Any brand that is nailing their marketing is showing potential clients that they genuinely care; that they understand them and clearly demonstrate that they can help. They take the time to create an incredible experience at each touch point of the customer's journey. They don't just talk about it they demonstrate it in everything that they do and deliver. This goes back to the discussion we had earlier about values – you are showing others what you believe in and drawing in those who believe it too.

Great marketeers are passionate story tellers and educators – they give away their expertise to help others in their content. In doing so, they further establish trust by showing up consistently, nurturing their audience so that they can create a group of raving fans. Fans who in time will turn to them when they have a need that the brand or person can solve.

*NOTE: Marketing is NOT just your social media. It provides opportunities both digitally and offline.*

Most businesses combine offline and online marketing methods in their strategy, although a higher percentage will lean towards digital marketing because of ideal client behaviours and because there is no denying the scope of its reach, speed and efficiency and often return on investment.

***That said, I have something very important to say.***

Spending hours scrolling on your social media and consuming content (unless it is strategically linked to research, or you are engaging with your ideal clients) does not demonstrate intentional and conscious leadership behaviour. Your return on 'time' investment if you are unintentionally scrolling will not be good. The next generation of CEO is not scrolling and consuming their feed unintentionally. Going down a rabbit hole will not grow your business! This behaviour will take you away from other revenue generating tasks that could create a much better return for you.

To help you decide which methods might suit your business, I have listed some different distribution channels that you might want to consider for your own marketing. Remember you don't have to do them all and they might not all be the right fit for you.

**Content Marketing**

Probably the best known and most used, this is content that is published in different ways to build brand awareness and nurture relationships with those in the red chairs (or to get them into the red chairs in the first place!). Some might refer to this as digital marketing, but content can be created offline too – blogs, vlogs, catalogues and various information.

**Social Media**

The most common channel used by businesses just starting out are the various social platforms. This has revolutionised marketing for small businesses because done right, it can bring in new leads for free or you can pay and tighten your targeting. You can also use these platforms for your content marketing. Please know that you do not own the connections that you build up here, the platforms do. If these platforms crash or you get hacked you risk losing your connections and your media/content too (if it's not banked elsewhere). It is advisable to diversify your risk by looking at various distribution channels to build your audience, as is protecting where you store your content too.

Combining content marketing on social media provides a brilliant opportunity for businesses. But adopting this as your only approach is risky, particularly without an intentional, measured strategy.

This risk is that you may fall into the spray and pray approach, posting random content and posts inconsistently without any real strategy then sitting and waiting for the clients to come (without any other sales or marketing activities alongside). Hoping and praying that someone will pick up the phone or land in your inbox wanting to work with you.

I see so many clients fall into this trap. I've also done it myself. It is exhausting and overwhelming and lacks flow because it often comes from a place of panic marketing. Better to take some time and know the results you are seeking from your content, so you can track and measure the insights and results to see if it is having the desired impact.

**Search Engine Optimisation (SEO)**

This is when you optimise the content on your website to make it more visible to search engines – the aim is to attract more traffic from searches made by your ideal customer.

**Search Engine Marketing**

This is also known as pay per click. These are those paid ads you see in Google and other platforms. Businesses pay to have a link to their site placed in a prominent position on search engine result pages. Each time the customer clicks on the link, you pay – whether the lead converts or not.

## Email Marketing

I advocate using email to create your own database of potential clients whom you nurture through your content to build those important relationships. Users sign up to your list through a subscription or opt in. One way to create an opt in is to offer them something valuable (either free or low cost) that they share their email address to access. Another way is to allow them to subscribe to your updates. Both options are a great way to grow your audience and nurture them providing you take the time to build the relationship through regular conversations.

### Retargeting

This is when you contact an existing or a potential customer who has previously interacted with you to get them to come back or convert them into a sale. Ways to do this include placing a paid advert on a social media newsfeed or retargeting them with a product/service that they have been looking at on your social channels or on your website.

You can also take a retargeted approach through your sales activities. This is when you follow up with those who have expressed an interest in working with you previously. To keep track of this, I suggest using a Customer Relationship Management (CRM) system or a project management tool so you can keep records of discussions and diarise follow ups.

### Affiliate/Influencer Marketing

Different but have similar approaches. Affiliate marketing is when you utilise others to market your product for you and they are paid for each customer who converts. Influencer marketing is when you utilise high profile brands or individuals who have a large following to promote your product or service. Normally you pay them to wear or showcase the product, rather than pay for the conversion of the sale.

There are additional sub types of marketing that can be broken down from each of these different approaches. Think outside of the box for your own business. Be strategic (as well as mindful of the best use of time and budget) in deciding the right marketing approach for you and your business. I don't advocate you use just one, but equally, when you are doing this alone, your budget (and time if doing it yourself) will not enable you to tackle them all well.

If you want to create a strong marketing strategy, pick the right approach for your specific business and situation, then form a plan which will integrate into your wider strategy. It is also important to test, monitor, tweak and make decisions on suitability as your business journey continues.

## Speaking Opportunities

Another way to reach your ideal client may be through offering trainings, presentations or attending events. By sharing a keynote presentation which showcases your knowledge to a group of potential ideal clients, you give yourself a great opportunity to create new leads into your own audience. When you do this, providing you have permission, don't forget to provide your contact details and/or a call to action, so that you give them reason to come into your world. Once again, your free offer or low-price product can be a great fit here.

## Your Content Marketing Messaging

Matching and positioning your messaging to your ideal client and their needs is a MUST. I have listed some quick tips to help you.

- Seek to understand, ask questions, listen and respond to needs in your content.
- Get good at demonstrating that what you sell is the answer to their problem.
- Get good at telling and sharing stories that your audience can relate to.
- Pay close attention to what your happy customers tell you and write about you.
- Be consistent – in this noisy world, your messaging needs to be clear, concise and be seen consistently so you are at the forefront of your ideal client's mind.
- Always talk directly to your ideal client.
- Demonstrate how you solve their problem.
- Remember, sell the transformation/destination to the right potential client – not the product itself. What will it give them?

A basic practice used by marketeers is the product, place, price and promotion model. The 'marketing mix', also known as the 4 Ps of marketing, is the foundation of your marketing plan. It represents the main decisions you will have to make when marketing your products or services:

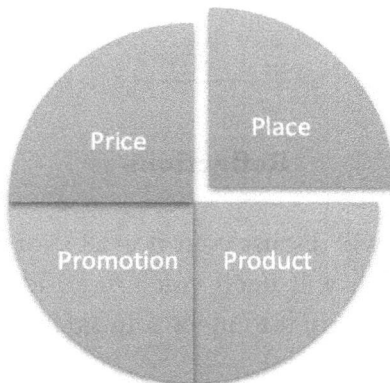

**Products** - the goods or services you offer to meet the needs of your customer. Product positioning is the marketing strategy used to help your goods or services and the relevant messaging become more easily known to your customers.

**Price** - the perceived value of your product. The amount a customer will pay to obtain the good or service. There are different pricing strategies to help draw customers to you over your competitor too.

**Place** – where will you reach your buyer? Where are they hanging out? Where can you best to show up for them? How will you become visible and create traffic into your red seats? Traffic is the volume of people who will notice your goods and services. This is CRITICAL. You can have the best product in the world, with the greatest value price but if you do not have an audience who you have credibility with, you will not drive them a step closer to buying from you.

**Promotion** – these are the tools you use to connect with your customer. PR can be radio/media articles. Personal outreach is direct reach to your warm ideal client. Sales promotions can be a short period of time to your ideal client. You can create a short-term price or added bonuses to help promote and achieve a sale.

### Reflections

In Question 8 we will discuss your overall strategy and plan but executing your plan will need you to consider the marketing and sales strategy within it to meet your goals.

Some questions to ask yourself for your marketing strategy: -

## What are your goals?

What do you want your business to achieve in the short and long term? You will have financial targets within this, but also consider your brand and its profile. If you want to increase awareness, what specific methods will you adopt to grow awareness and start to fill those red seats?

## Have you done your research?

Have you nailed your ideal client profile? Are you crystal clear on them and what they need and want from you? Is your messaging positioned right for them and are they responding?

## Who else does what you do?

Don't get bogged down looking left and right or going down a rabbit hole as it will slow you down. But do take some time checking out your competitors. What are they doing to market themselves? How are your ideal clients responding to them? What can you learn from them? What needs to change for you?

## What is unique about you?

Why you? Why would I come and buy from you over your competitor? What makes you special? What needs to come across in your messaging to help your clients realise this?

## Where will you show up and how often?

These days a blend of offline and online methods is used. You need to firstly understand your audience and where they are likely to hang out and you need to go meet them there. What platforms and methods will enable you to reach them in a way that they understand, value and answers their questions?

## How are you selling?

Sales is about taking the potential lead and building the relationship to move them a step closer to buying. It is important to build close relationships. Your marketing process and insights support this.

As an owner managed business, I have already outlined that it is probable you will take control of both marketing and sales initially. Therefore, it is important you understand that your lead generation is integral to your sales conversions (conversions are how many you take to the next step of your sales process and thereon to become a customer).

If you have a lack of clients, it is important to find out exactly why and address this. Often it isn't that you are not converting the sale, but that you don't have enough leads coming into the sales pipeline in the first place. This means that it isn't the sales process that is the issue, but the marketing process (or additional sales activities) that is creating a bottleneck. Knowing the difference helps you take the RIGHT action to resolve it.

The other challenge I see (and resonate with) is that there is often fear attached to marketing and sales activities, largely because promoting your own brand makes you feel vulnerable and opens fears of rejection. I know this can be hard. However, I must be honest. If this is something you are experiencing and it is causing you to stall, I urge you to get support to work through any blocks that may be stopping you taking action. Remember the rowing boat going round and round? All the strategy and knowledge in the world won't drive you forward if you are getting in your own way because you are fearful of the execution. As I said before, your head in the sand won't work; you cannot ignore these important activities. Without marketing and sales, you will NOT have a business.

The Head of Marketing (you or whomever you hire in) has the important job of analysing facts and feedback from your audience. The same applies to your Head of Sales. Get clear on the objectives, understand the numbers that are coming into your sales pipeline, and seek to understand what is working well and what needs to improve so conversions are higher and buying decisions quicker. Review the successes and learnings at each stage.

## Do you know your conversions?

It is vitally important to know what sales you are aiming for and the steps you will take to get there (your sales process). To see what is working, you should track and monitor progress and tweak as needed.

### For example

If you put ten quality leads into your sales process and two of them convert to a sale, you know that 20% is your conversion rate. This data is important to you for future targets, as is where these two converted leads came from so you can focus there to get more.

If you want ten future clients, you will need a minimum of fifty into your pipeline to hit your numbers based on this 20% conversion rate.

The question should then be how do you get fifty into your pipeline? What has worked before? Where do your leads generally come from? How could you get more? What appointments do you have in your diary that will enable you to get these fifty in so you can move them through the process to convert ten new clients? What is it that you do that leads to your best conversions?

If you don't have these insights because you are just starting out or haven't monitored, I urge you to test and take action, monitor and track the result so you can see where to best focus your energy moving forward to get your greatest return on investment.

Armed with this knowledge, you should then put in place consistent marketing and sales activities that you action each day and week that will lead to you getting fifty leads into your pipeline that you then put through the process and move to converting 20% so you get your ten new clients for the quarter.

I am firm believer that your sales activities are as important as your marketing. In the early stages of building your business you should focus more on this, because marketing isn't an overnight success and momentum takes time to build.

There are many ways you can generate sales quickly into your business. I have listed some ideas below to help if you are feeling stuck.

1. Build the relationship. Don't just reach out to people when you are selling something. Take the time to check in on them, nurture the relationship, build the trust.
2. When the time is right, don't be afraid to ask directly for the sale. Just do it in the right way. Who do you already know that your product is a great fit for? Why not ask them directly? Invite them to take a look? Many of my clients are grateful for this because

otherwise they may not have known that the opportunity to work with me was there.

3. What about asking anyone you already know if they know of anyone who might be a fit for the product that you are selling? It is wonderful to receive referrals as they are often warmer leads than those who you otherwise would need time to nurture from cold.

4. Take an interest. Ask questions, learn about your audience and when they tell you that they want/need something, respond accordingly.

5. Remember to include a call to action in your communication with them.

6. Who has mentioned to you previously that they would love to work with you? Why not check if now is the right time? The fortune is in the follow up. TOO many give up after the second, third or fourth no/not the right time response. If you set this up right, although it can take months or years to be the right time, one day it may well be. But if you give up, the sale will never come.

7. Ask for and share testimonials from your clients for trust and proof.

8. Ask your clients if they know anyone that could be a fit. They love your products already. You could look to incentivise or reward them for the referral.

9. Create a low-priced product that enables your customer to get a taster of your offering without a giant leap to buy immediately. This is a great way to build credibility, demonstrate your value and get more testimonials.

10. Acknowledge a referral. Be thankful for a testimonial. Honour someone space to consider your opportunity. Treat others how you would like to be treated. But do

NOT avoid asking just because they may say no. They might, but they also might say yes.

*TIP: Get Phil M Jones in your world! His book, Exactly What to Say is a MUST for your library. He is brilliant at sales conversations.*

### Do you value your clients?

Acquisition of clients can be costly in cash and time. Therefore, it is worth looking at ways to offer additional products and up sells to your existing clients alongside new client strategy so you extend the lifetime value of your customers.

Your value ladder is key to this as you listen, respond and provide additional products for your clients that mean you can continue to support their needs. How else can you help and support them? What is it that they need for their next step with you?

How you onboard your clients and deliver will contribute to their overall experience and retention with you. Ensure that you have in place check in points at the start, middle and end of their journey to keep the channels of communication open. Gather feedback so you can continually develop the relationship, improve the experience and value, and look at additional ways to retain and support them.

The critical component here is to put as much attention into retaining your existing clients and improving their experience as the effort you make to develop new clients. Remember that it isn't just about retaining them. They are the ambassadors for you and their loyalty will open the doors for additional opportunities with new clients through referrals.

## What is in your funnel?

Digital marketing helps you understand your customers further and build better relationships with them on a larger scale.

The digital space gives you more opportunity to collect data from your audience about their behaviours and interactions. Which in turn can help you gather greater insights into what your ideal client needs from you.

A concept adopted in the digital marketing space is the sales funnel. Done right this can create an automated marketing machine (alongside your own manual marketing and sales activities) for your business.

This image below is taken from Shutterstock.

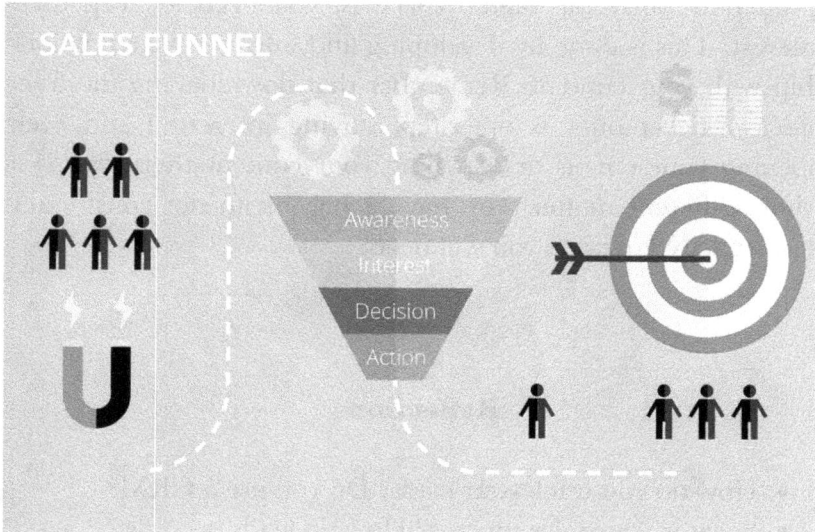

To the left you see a magnet.

Your free offer and low-price product can help you attract and draw in potential clients and leads (think red seats...) into the top of your funnel. These offers could be a free or low-priced PDF, training, swipe file, eBook or even a paid advert. It needs to be something of value to your ideal client to incentivise them to get into your world, provide you with their details, get into the top of your funnel and onto your email list.

The idea is that this is automated. So, a series of welcome emails is provided when the individual signs up to the lead magnet so you can nurture and start to build a relationship with them at each step of the journey through the funnel.

Irrespective of how they come into your funnel, you have a series of steps to take them through to help them move from prospect to buyer. Awareness is just the start of the process and given how noisy the digital space is, you need to keep their interest. This is done by developing and nurturing the relationship with your content. Remember that downloading the freebie/low ticket offer is one step, staying interested and even opening your emails or watching your content thereafter is a whole different matter. You have a big job to do; consistency and tenacity are traits you will need.

## Reflections

- How do you track your leads? Do you use a CRM?
- What is your sales process? How do leads become aware of your business and how do they move through to buy from you?
- How could you create this process into an automated digital funnel?

- Where are the opportunities to build awareness of your brand and offering?
- What are your conversion rates? Where are your highest conversions coming from? What can you learn from this?
- Where else could you generate leads?
- What offers could you create as lead magnets?
- What are the holes in your boat that need plugging?
- What are the patterns and insights you can gather to improve the whole experience?
- Where are you leaving money on the table right now?

———

# 7

# HOW CLOSE ARE YOU TO YOUR NUMBERS?

---

**"Revenue is one thing, it is what you have left at the end that counts."**

— BEN BARKER

---

A wise man, Ben Barker once said to me "revenue is one thing, it is what you have left that counts". Which leads us nicely onto step 4 of my framework – Profit.

You have heard the age old saying, 'money doesn't buy you happiness', but I fly the flag that it does afford you the luxury of greater choices and allows you to make an even greater impact on the world around you too.

Money also helps your shoulders relax, takes the noose from your neck and keeps the wolves from the door. When you have enough to hit your basic needs and put food on the table (and in the case of your business cover its basic operating expenses and pay you a salary), you can sleep at night.

The most common causes of insolvency in business come from inadequate cashflow, poor strategic management and poor financial control. I promise that when you get up close and personal with your numbers (as hard as it may feel), set up a business model that is right for you and where appropriate (and wanted), access recurring revenue streams (or at least have a much better handle on managing your cashflow and profit), it really changes the game for you.

The financial aspirations and targets your business set are unique to you. Irrespective of what they are, if you are serious about laying foundations and building a business for growth, you need to get close and meaningful with your numbers and become the Financial Director for your business (or, just like marketing and sales, you need to hire in someone to do it for you).

If this question and topic gives you jitters, that is the exact reason you need to dive into it. You, me – we've work to do together!

No more head in the sand. Yep, I know it feels safer. But I assure you it will not work or serve you or your business. Every day you keep your head in there, you are giving your business one less chance to succeed. For every business owner I have helped lift their chin and uncover their eyes, the pain has been worth it when they face their reality and take the right action to improve.

If you are starting from ground zero, then let's first cover off some basic terms and jargon that you need to understand. (If you are on top of this, feel free to skip on past...)

## Revenue and Cashflow

Revenue is the money that your company generates from a sale of your product or service (irrespective of receipt into your bank). Cashflow is the actual cash you physically receive as a deposit into your bank (inflow) or you pay for an expense and the money leaves your account (outflow).

No business can afford to ignore its cashflow. Monitoring this should be like cleaning your teeth. A crucial health habit for your business.

Positive cashflow means your business will be able to settle its bills and invest in its growth. A negative cashflow means you'll need to find an alternative source of income to be able to pay off your debts and operating expenses.

This is particularly relevant to product-based businesses.

## As an example:

- Your product goes through a lengthy sales chain and some of your wholesale customers don't pay their invoices for 120 days.
- You still make a good profit on the products, but you don't have the physical cash readily available.
- Your suppliers expect to be paid every 15 or 30 days.
- Even though you have made the sale (and the revenue), you won't have the physical cash you need to pay the suppliers for materials. This could risk your ability to operate and manufacture more of the products to generate sales.
- Even though your unit sales are increasing and profitable, you won't get paid in time to pay your suppliers, meet payroll and pay other operational

expenses. If you cannot meet your financial obligations in a timely way, your creditors may force you into bankruptcy at a period when sales are growing rapidly.

*Hence why cashflow is critical to your business.*

## Breaking Even

When your company breaks even, it is the point at which your total revenue is equal to your costs or expenses. This is useful for you to see the minimum number of sales or units you need to make to avoid a loss.

## Profit

In the traditional sense of accounting, profit is the result of your revenue, minus your expenses. There are two areas to focus on, the gross profit, which is revenue minus the direct costs of the goods (COGS), and the net profit, which is revenue minus the deduction of all business expenses (including your COGS).

It is advisable to also know the profit margins within your business. This enables you to see how profitable each of your products is individually and your business overall. To work out your margins for each product, divide your gross (or net) profit by your total sales and multiple by 100 to provide a %.

All these are important numbers to understand. Cashflow (inflow and outflow) shows how well your company is managing its cash position and how well you can meet your operating expenses and debt obligations. However, it is what is left at the end (profit) which will determine the success of your business, therefore thinking in terms of profitability is critical.

Throughout my career I worked with this traditional P&L (profit and loss) accounting method, but things changed for me in my own business when I discovered a new methodology called Profit First.

### Would you like Profit First?

---

"Most of us want to live a lifestyle of comfort without worry."

"Profit is not an event, it is a habit."

— MIKE MICHALOWICZ

---

I first discovered *Profit First* when I read a book by its creator, Mike Michalowicz (go check him out, his work is incredible – www.mikemichalowzicz.com/profit-first). Then a friend and colleague of mine, Claire Sweet of Peace Together Money Coaching, summarised the basic components in a training she delivered for my clients.

The premise of *Profit First* is that Mike is on a mission to eradicate entrepreneurship poverty. He believes that the greatest source of entrepreneurial stress is the lack of cash reserves (which I concur with). He talks about entrepreneurs starting with a vision for financial freedom (yep). But often the reality is that you are undercharging for your products or do not have enough cashflow and profit in your business as a reserve and buffer. His approach suggests that if, after putting a small amount aside for profit (FIRST), you do not have enough left to cover your operating expenses, you have a problem. The problem is that you cannot sustainably afford to run your business. You therefore need to take decisive action to either increase your sales (more volume or higher prices) or reduce your costs.

The method he shares rips up the rule book of the traditional approach, putting profit aside after sales and before you allow your business to use what it has left for expenses.

$$\text{Sales} - \textbf{Profit} = \text{Expenses.}$$

It was as if a lightbulb had gone on above my head. I resonated immediately. I had always been a fan of setting up savings pots in my personal account (my Mum taught me this through her own saving behaviours). I know that psychologically if I leave money in my account, I will spend it, whereas when I put the money immediately to one side in a separate pot, I cannot see it and therefore I work with what I have, spending within my means. I have saved for many things over the years with this approach as the pot that is put to one side gradually, like a compound effect, starts to grow.

This is how *Profit First* works in your business. You build it in a similar way (and it suggests you include other pots too - VAT, Tax, Budgets; you get to choose). You then keep it where you save it or, as Mike does, move it into your personal account every ninety days as a performance bonus and reward for your hard work. Your approach will be unique to you (I personally like seeing mine grow and it inspires me to put more in there too!)

*Profit First* focuses on the principle of behavioural psychology that you spend what you have available only. It is an incredible principle for forward planning and budgeting too and I am so passionate about its impact that I bring in an expert to teach this to my clients who go through my Get Set for Success™ LIVE programme.

## How much do you value your time?

Before we dive deeper on this, I want to shout it loud. You MUST pay yourself!

Even if your salary starts low and you have a strategy for how this will increase over time, it is imperative that you draw something from your business from the start. This is irrespective of whether you are set up as a Ltd or a sole trader business.

When I work with my clients and we dive into their numbers, one of the very first facts I want to understand (alongside their revenue and profit) – is what they pay themselves for the work that they do in their business.

If you are just starting out, you might intentionally decide to draw a very small salary and this may equate to a 'time value by the hour' which is much lower than you are used to.

However, if you don't pay yourself, don't track your salary and don't know the margins of your products, when we shine a light on your numbers, we might discover that you are a) working for a shockingly low amount b) worse still, volunteering as the CEO of your business.

I know it can be hard to hear this. I have made the same screw ups myself. However, it is only after these difficult and honest conversations that the reality hits home, the fire is lit and change can come.

Let me give you an example of valuing your time as well as making a profit. For the purpose of this exercise I have worked in British Pounds.

- You run a cake business.
- You charge £100 to make one cake.
- The ingredients cost you £20 and therefore you have a healthy profit of £80 and 80% profit margin.
- However, it takes you three days (17 hours) to make the cake.
- Therefore, you are essentially earning £80 divided by 17 = £4.70 an hour for your time.

When working out your pricing strategy, you need to include your time in your considerations. Doing this will help you understand if you are happy with the return you receive for the time you give. If you are not yet you continue to do it, what do you think will happen over time?

I can tell you. Unintentionally continuing without this knowledge will mean you will come to resent your business. You will resent your clients and start to question if it is worth it. Equally, your numbers may not add up for you. You started for financial freedom and your business model isn't enabling you to work towards this.

Valuing your time also incorporates your boundaries (as per your personal contract). However, for the purpose of this question, I encourage you to focus on the insights you can gather from looking at the physical numbers to see that you are being paid according to your value and time. When you know the reality, you can see where the opportunities to improve are.

Pricing is a question I get asked a lot. It is impossible for me to give you an exact science for your own pricing strategy in this book, as I believe it is unique to your own needs, experience, industry, ideal client and how you and your client currently value and perceive your time to be worth.

What I can do is give you some prompts to work out what value you are going to place on your time, so that you can start to audit and review your current pricing to see where your gaps may be.

Please know that I am personally not an advocate of my business model being one where I exchange time for money. However, you may be (it is important to work out what is right for you) and these prompts are helpful if you, like me, sell packages and programmes too, because a basic understanding of what your time is worth by the hour/day helps you price out your products correctly to meet your need as well as your clients.

- What is your revenue (or profit) goal for the year?
- How many weeks do you want to work?
- How many hours a week do you physically want to work (or delivering for clients), depending on the role you are taking in your business.
- For example - £100,000 / 37 weeks / 20 hours = £135 per hour. This means to meet your £100k target, you will need to physically work and create revenue that equates to around £135 per hour.
- If you are currently charging out £50 an hour, then you will need to work more than double the hours you want to achieve your target. The numbers just don't add up. Something needs to change: either the pricing strategy, the revenue target or the number of hours you are prepared to work. The greater the insight, the better the opportunity to find a solution.

Another point to consider is, if you know your net profit margin is 50%, then your goal of £100,000 banked in profit is in fact £200,000 in revenue. This then changes the prompts above again.

Likewise, if you only want to physically serve clients for ten hours a week, then you know your value per hour needs to double.

I always advise you do this with consideration to your industry norms. However, don't let your belief systems stop you charging your worth. Take into consideration the perceived value of your offer to your ideal client. Price only becomes an issue for your ideal client when they don't perceive the value as worth the investment.

You may need to start smaller and work up. I am a huge advocate of a £99 offer to build your credibility and testimonials. As your client list grows so can your prices.

Pricing strategies should therefore consider your experience, perceived value (are you wanting to position yourself as high value like a supermarket own brand product or high quality like a luxury watch brand) and costs, so you can ensure your margins are right and the timescales of your cash flowing in versus out can meet your expenses as well as pay you properly and in line with the value of your time.

*NOTE: Always be considerate to your clients if you plan to change your pricing. Look at an appropriate communication strategy to do this.*

## What about cashflow forecasting?

Remember, being profitable does not automatically mean you have adequate cashflow in your business.

A cashflow forecast will help you discover the future balance in your bank account at any given time and assist with making informed decisions in your business. Cash forecasting may be required if you are looking to banks or investors for investment, loans or overdrafts too. Whether you are a sole trader or a Ltd company, forecasting is a useful tool.

## Why is it helpful?

- Helps you forecast (predict) what is going to happen to cashflow to make sure your business can survive (and thrive)
- Makes sure you can afford to pay suppliers and employees (and covers basic operating expenses)
- Helps you predict and plan for growth (this feeds into your marketing and sales strategy)

## What are the challenges with it?

- You cannot forecast for unforeseen factors (like a global pandemic)
- You forecast with often limited information
- It is at best an estimate

In addition to cash forecasting is your sales forecasting. They work in tandem. You would aim to run your management reports weekly (or track manually depending on where you are on your journey of systems and processes being in place). What you need to do is measure how you are performing (actual sales or cashflow that you generated) versus the forecast you set.

For example. You forecast sales of £6000 in month 1. You make a new sale of £5000 in month 1 (being paid in two instalments of £2500) and you have recurring cashflow of £2000 as well. This makes your actual sales for month 1: £5000 + £2000 = £7000 so you are up £1000 actual sales versus your forecast. However, your actual cashflow is £2500 + £2000 = £4500 against a cashflow forecast of £5000, so you are actually £500 behind target.

Even if forecasting is an estimate, it is better than no estimate at all.

### Reflections

- How do you currently track your numbers?
- What are your current operating expenses?
- What revenue are you generating? How regular is this? Do you have gaps month to month which mean you cannot pay your expenses or your salary?
- What are your profit margins overall and by product? Which products are your most profitable? Do you want to continue offering them?
- When you reflect on the value of your time, are you happy with the return you get for the time you invest in the creation and delivery of your products?
- How regularly are you putting cash reserves aside for budgeting, profit, tax, VAT and contingency?
- How do you feel overall about your financials in the business?
- What needs to improve?

# 8

# HOW STRATEGIC IS YOUR PLAN?

---

**"Rowing harder doesn't help if the boat is headed in the wrong direction."**

— KENICHI OHMAE

---

The fifth and final step in my framework is the plan.

When I first mention strategy, I often see a blank expression from clients or panic as the word feels corporate, complex and sometimes out of reach.

I am going to share a secret with you - it really isn't.

Strategy is simply your master plan to move forward. It is the intended direction in your business and the exact actions that you will take to get there, along with how you mobilise the resources you'll need to execute it (and review and prepare for risks along the way).

## Some points useful to understand: -

- A goal is your intended destination - the overall result you are looking to achieve. I am sure you have heard of keeping your goals SMART (specific, measurable, achievable, realistic and time scaled). For example: Achieve £100k in total sales by X date. I am all about keeping things realistic, but with a little stretch included too!

- An objective is a step of action you intend to take to reach that goal. You might have three objectives that need to be achieved in quarter 1 to be moving towards the year end goal of £100k in total sales. These may be four new 1:1 clients by X date, thirty new members into a membership by X date and the launch of a new lead magnet by X date.

- Another misconception is the Key Performance Indicator (KPI). Take it from someone who runs her business her way; some of the corporate experience and knowledge you have is worth its weight in gold and fully transferrable into your business. KPIs especially! It is a useful numeric measure of performance for any activity that's important to your business. These are metrics that you really care about, but a metric is any number that you track. For example: you have a goal of five new clients. Your stats show for every presentation you give to your ICA, you will convert two new clients. Therefore, you know that to achieve your goal you need to deliver a minimum of three presentations. This can then become a KPI that you track to ensure you are on track to achieve your goal.

- We have already discussed forecasting which is another important measure. It is a prediction of what you will achieve (normally in sales/cashflow). This is also integral in how you set targets for yourself and plan your strategy.
- By using metrics (targets, KPIs, forecasting) - you can plan a pretty accurate picture of performance for your company should you hit ALL, some or none of your targets.

---

Your strategy starts with the vision and intention of where you want to end up. Mine typically will commence with my financial goal. What is it that I want to achieve by the end of the year? I then reverse engineer from this point to map out the steps needed to get there. This is simply the practice of beginning with the end in mind and working backwards to see what you need to do to make your vision/goal(s) a reality.

Common obstacles that cause business owners to stall are not seeing the vision or a lack of clarity on the exact steps (and commitment of action) to get there. Your execution is as important as your visualisation. Once again, if you struggle with the implementation of making your vision come to life, it may be that this becomes a potential hire in the future into your team. This is where operational roles can really make a difference.

*Will It Make my Boat Go Faster* by Harriet Beveridge and Ben Hunt is a brilliant book (and question) that I refer to when I work with my clients. I was fortunate to hear Ben Davies speak on stage and the impact of the question has never left me.

Ben was on the British Olympic Rowing Team in 2000 and the story of how they achieved their gold medal is inspiring. The book shares strategies to achieving your own gold medal, but it is the power of the question that I love the most.

It forces you to get your blinkers on and be laser focused on your greatest priority today, tomorrow and next week to action. In the case of the British Rowing Team, if they were tempted to make bad food choices, they would ask themselves, "If I eat this, will it make my boat go faster?" It is a great way to bring your subconscious into the conscious and be mindful in the steps you do or don't take.

This practice starts by knowing your destination, then getting clear on the actions you are committed to take which will move you in the right direction. Then it is about accountability to these actions and the successful habits and routines to adopt to keep you on track. Check and measure that you are staying accountable, are making informed decisions and measuring progress, so that you can make headway in your own boat going faster.

Use an analogy of your holiday as an example.

- The destination you want to travel to is the goal.
- You research it and make sure it is where you want to go.
- You get excited, connected and passionate about getting there.
- You start at the destination and work backwards (reverse engineer), breaking down the actions to arrive.
- These actions are the steppingstones (objectives) that you would set to achieve your goal.
- If you don't set the steps and you don't take the action

to get there, then you won't arrive at the holiday destination you have your heart set on.

- Along the way, things may change. You might need to change your travel option; fly to a different airport – it may be that you change your mind about the destination. Things change, journeys need to be agile. Measuring your progress, adjusting the journey and staying accountable is you 'making your boat go faster' to reach the dream destination you have set yourself.

As a CEO of your business, you should know exactly what you are selling, launching, promoting each day, week and month. You (and your team) should know what the priorities are in your business so that you can sense check that your actions are making your boat go faster towards achieving them.

Waking up and not knowing what you are doing day-to-day isn't the way to lead your business. This is winging it (remember this will only work for so long). When you know what you are focused on, it will enable you to get yourself into a state of productive flow as you focus on the specific action that you (or your team) need to take to move one step closer to the next milestone and the vision becomes even clearer along the way.

When you have the plan clarified, each week and day, you can get clear on what your priorities are. Ask yourself, is this the most important task I need to undertake today? Will this help my business ring the till? Will it make the right impact? Will it make my boat go faster?

I urge my clients to schedule regular strategy days (minimum annually, otherwise every six months). If you work alone, you might want to do these with a colleague or hire someone to support you with this process. For my strategy days, I like to take myself away from the office and hire somewhere for a few days in the quiet countryside, so I can get creative and focus on what matters most.

I also recommend scheduling CEO days each month or a minimum each quarter to enable you to proactively review your business performance and make changes to the plan accordingly. You need to make time in your diary (with your team if you have one) to evaluate your progress. What is going well? Are you hitting the targets set? If not, why not? What needs to change or be adjusted? This review process is important so that you can be agile and tweak your steps depending on external and internal circumstances to still meet your goals.

When you review your strategic plan, you're looking at the assumptions made and checking to see where your business stands in relation to those assumptions. What you thought would be challenges and threats to your business a year ago may not be now. Don't be afraid to change any part of the strategic plan. If outside factors are having a bigger impact on your business than you initially thought, you may have to change your objectives or goals.

A global pandemic was a prime example of agility in planning and forecast, unprecedented in terms of its global impact. But, however devastating its blow, there is a well-known saying that was adopted by many businesses around the world as they navigated it:

NECESSITY IS THE MOTHER OF ALL INVENTION.

Back to my earlier point about crisis often being the catalyst to positive change – this was indeed the case for many during this difficult time.

It was an opportunity to re-evaluate the need of the customer. A chance to pivot a business strategy and many new businesses were born. What was apparent was the need for an open mind, creativity, resilience, a backup plan and some grit and tenacity to embrace the change needed to reframe the mind and see the opportunity.

Planning is important. But equally important is action. They work in tandem to make progress happen (we will discuss this in Question 9).

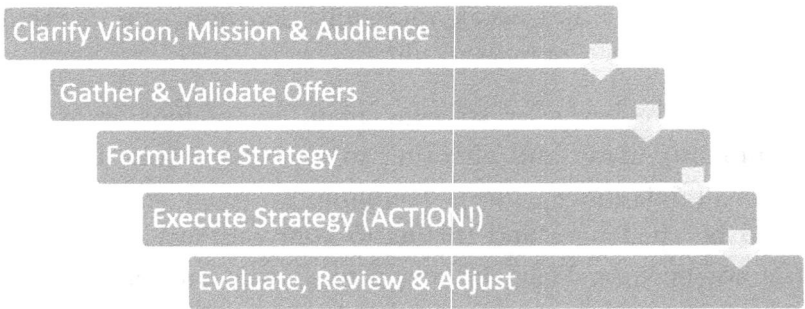

Clarify Vision, Mission & Audience

Gather & Validate Offers

Formulate Strategy

Execute Strategy (ACTION!)

Evaluate, Review & Adjust

The steps to achieving your strategy are outlined in the figure above. Ensure that your vision is clear, your purpose (and why) is compelling enough to motivate you into action and you have clarity on who your ideal client is.

The more you seek to understand from your ideal client, the more you can gather the products and services you want to offer them. It is important to validate these offers to ensure they meet the needs of your client.

It is also important to point out at this stage that the most elaborate plan cannot save you if you never ACT on it (more on this in Question 9). Often, I see (and have been guilty of myself at times) the following behaviours: -

- Lots of planning without movement
- Obsession over minor details
- Projects abandoned, unfinished
- Living so much in the future, trying to pre-plan every eventuality
- Over consuming (remember the 'I need to know how...')

These behaviours are often rooted in fear and misalignment. The fear takes hold and keeps you still. Procrastination becomes real as you do other things that keep your rowing boat going in circles and then frustration kicks in. None of this pays the bills and it won't get you closer to your goals.

If you find yourself here, please go back to Question 1 and dig deep into the actions I recommend there.

The greatest and most successful leaders on this planet have one thing in common. They take QUICK, DECISIVE action every single time. If you struggle with this, I urge you to look at how you can improve. Or look at who you need to hire into your team as an operator to execute the ideas and vision that you have. Standing still and procrastinating is not an option if you want to succeed and grow.

### What are the steps to yours?

Your strategy doesn't have to be complicated. In fact, the simpler you can keep it the more chance you've got to keep it alive. I want you to get into a routine of working strategically, having the detail you need at your fingertips to review day-to-day.

As you become more strategic with your leadership of your business and you hold regular strategy and CEO days, you will know this information already because you regularly review.

However, for the purpose of this first strategy, put aside a week or at least two days out of your diary so that you can focus on this exercise.

1. Start by thinking of your financial goal. Where are you heading? (B)

2. Then review where you are now (A) and where you have been. Reflect on what has gone well, what products have sold well, what opportunities and lessons you have learnt. What have you enjoyed? What is causing you problems? Get clear on the specific wins and progress you have made and the holes that remain in your boat.

3. Consider your product mix and business model (review your value ladder too). If you continue as you are, will you achieve your financial goal? If not, what do you need to sell more of? Improve, change or even remove and replace? What new products would you like to introduce that your customers are telling you they need or want?

4. Consider what revenue you have predicted in your forecast already so you can work out the gaps to close.

5. Crunch the numbers so you are creating a draft forecast of what products you need to sell to hit your target.

6. Then start to break down these products so you are clear when you intend to launch/promote/sell them. Then you reverse engineer these so you can see what actions need to happen in your marketing, sales and audience size to enable you to hit the goals.

7. Get clear on any upcoming costs and your standard operating expenses. Look at your profit margins and make sure you are happy with these in your individual products.

*NOTE: If you don't have this level of detail about where you are heading, I suggest you look firstly at your financial target you have for the year, then break this down by quarter and month. What new sales do you need to achieve? How many? What revenue targets do you have? The key is that you have some realistic goals in mind that you are committed to working towards so that you can start to break down the strategy.*

8. Forecasting for new product launches or sales should work in conjunction with your personal contract where possible. My personal contract includes not working school holidays. Therefore, my delivery of products needs to ensure I can meet this requirement and any new products/promotions/launches must sit outside of this timeframe (unless I have team that can lead the marketing and sales activity on my behalf). Ensure you block out unavailable time.

9. Then it is time to break down the detail into a calendar over the next twelve months. As someone who is visual, I prefer to do this on flip chart or A3 paper or a white board. But you (like many of my clients) might prefer to use an online tool such as Asana or Trello, Excel or Word. Be sure to add in your unavailable time here too. As I don't work during August, this gets removed from my plan, although I still include any important actions here that my team are leading on my behalf. As you evolve your business and team, you can involve them in this exercise so that you all have access to the main strategy and each individual and team has their own too.

The idea is that you map out your strategy and objectives like you would a project. If there are ten actions you need to take to achieve your goal, then when do those ten actions need to be completed to achieve that goal? Include the detail of your sales and marketing strategy within this plan to achieve this too. This should also include your KPI metrics.

For example, if you know that you want five new clients in March and the marketing activities must be completed in January, then allocate this in your calendar.

If you are launching a new product in June and you have a twelve-week lead time to make sure the launch is a success, map this into your plan.

You can then tie this into the KPI metrics we discussed earlier. What are the most important actions you need to take to make sure the key goals are achieved? Perhaps you are solely responsible for the growth of your audience, and this is critical for the launch of your product. Therefore, you could look at the actions involved in making this happen as one or more of your KPIs.

10. Once you have plotted the detail across the year, you can break the action down in even more detail by quarter (ninety-day chunks).

11. Each ninety days, be clear on what your priority actions are and goals you are looking to achieve. Get clear on the KPIs to make them happen. You can break this down further into your thirty-day period and subsequently into weekly and daily actions and goals.

Make sure the goals are SMART; specific, can be measured, you have clear timescales attached, they are stretching but realistic (with the resources you have in place), and always consider the exact steps to implement and execute the plan. Also consider what could get in your way, the resources and support you will need and how you will stay accountable.

If you have team members, I encourage you to involve them in this process or at the very least ensure you communicate your intentions and plans as part of a cascade process. You want to ensure you take them along on the journey with you and keep them informed. Feeling part of it is important for them and you.

### How often do you recognise progress?

I champion my clients to hold up the mirror to recognise progress regularly. In business, you may find yourself focused on what hasn't worked out, the goals you didn't quite hit. (This is natural, by the way, as we are all programmed with a negative bias - it is what kept us safe in cave men and women days!) Anyway, my point is, if you hang around with me for long enough, I will get you shouting out your wins and celebrating your progress.

When I worked with *Yum!* recognition was ingrained in the culture. It was normal practice to celebrate each other, to call out and recognise progress and wins. Yet, I quickly realised this isn't normal for most.

*What gets recognised gets repeated.*

I encourage you to adopt this approach with your team, peers, colleagues, audience, clients and of course with yourself. One way to do this for you is to connect a goal you have to something that you would love to reward yourself with.

When I first started employment with Iceland as their Recruitment Officer, my boss talked about the 10% bonus I was entitled to receive if my performance hit the mark.

Together we broke down every 1-2% within that 10% and

linked them to the specific goals and KPIs that we agreed were the most important for me.

I have worked to many performance bonuses in employment and never had I felt as compelled to achieving my objectives.

Guess what… I smashed them all. 10% was mine!

My point here is you feel more motivated to taking action when the goal is so compelling and you have attached a reward to it.

At one point in my journey, I added in a product that wasn't in the strategy.

I said to my boys that if I achieved it, I would use the money from the sale and hire a beautiful venue with private pool, gaming room and land. I showed them the venue, I put down a deposit and I tracked every single sale that came through against the cost of it. It kept me focused, accountable and I was completely emotionally connected to making it happen.

Guess what… I hit my goal.

When I am emotionally connected to a goal, I am much more likely to do what it takes to make it happen. If I am vague about it, it may slip through the net. Linking your goal to a reward is a great way to motivate yourself and hold up the mirror and recognise your achievements along the way.

This approach and creating a culture of recognition is a brilliant way to bring your team along with you as you start to hire too.

So, to wrap up this part of our discussion, strategy doesn't have to be scary, unachievable, or difficult. Think of it like a project or planning a holiday. Set your destination, then break down the actions you need to take to map out the journey to get there. Then make it happen. Which leads me nicely onto the next step of our time together – action!

---

## Reflections

- How could you make time in your diary for strategy and CEO days?
- What insights do you have of your business and its strategy right now?
- What is going well?
- What needs to change?
- What would you like to achieve in the next 6-12 months?
- What steps do you need to take to get there?
- How could you make the goal more compelling by attaching a reward for achieving it?

---

# 9

# HOW READY ARE YOU FOR ACTION?

**"You'll never plough a field by turning it over in your mind."**

— IRISH PROVERB

Following the previous step in my framework (planning), it is time to make it happen with your actions!

As you become the CEO of your choosing, one thing is a given - you need to be leading it from the front.

Successful high performing leaders take BIG decisive Action. They are courageous, quick to act, take calculated risks and get more done than your average person in the same amount of time. This amounts to the speed of their decision making. They do not procrastinate.

If you want to grow as the leader of your business, you must develop your courage, intentionality and speed to act.

It starts by believing it can be done. Remember the Push Pull Formula: M=bp2.

Big Leaders don't try. They do it, or they do not.

I explained this recently to my son after he had a fall on his bike after half-heartedly attempting a small jump in the woods. When show jumping or eventing my horses, I wouldn't go at a fence with an 'I will give it a try' attitude. I had to see myself jumping it. I had to believe I could do it before I did. However nervous I was, I used my adrenaline to go ALL in at the fence because the horse would know whether I believed I could do it. Accidents and errors are more likely when you come from a place of 'I will try.' The same applies with any top sports performer. Half an effort is what will occur with an 'I will give it a try.' The intention isn't there and therefore the motivation as per the formula will be limited, which means so will your outcome be.

**You ready to go BIG or stay home?**

I want to talk to you about your productive flow as this is where your highest performance will come from. But before I do, I would like to address a fundamental starting point.

- Your mindset plays a big part in your results.
- Your mindset (beliefs about your potential and the quality of the ideas you have) will impact the actions that you take. This in turn will impact the outcomes you achieve (what you earn, the way your business runs and the time freedom you do/don't have.)

- Your thoughts impact your feelings which in turn impact your behaviour. This is integral to why you may not be acting decisively.

I'll bet a giant reason you're not taking BIG ACTION right now is because you are in your own way.

Telling yourself all sorts of reasons why you CANNOT do this. Getting distracted by menial jobs because they are safer than the BIG action you should be taking. Busy being busy.

I am not disputing that you may need deeper support in conquering this. But there are a couple of ways that you can start to address some of these mind demons, get more productive, more focused and start improving your habits/discipline right away if you want to.

There isn't any point setting goals and not acting on them. Let's start to look at how you could help yourself into a better, higher performing state of flow and productivity. Let's look at how you could smash some of those negative thoughts that tell you that you cannot do it.

To get yourself in the highest performing state, you need to work in flow.

### What is working in flow?

It is when your attention is heightened towards one task. Your creativity when in a flow state is effortless and you give yourself the best opportunity to perform at your best.

When in a state of flow, you will work intensely and mindfully to the task at hand and forget everything outside of it.

When your attention and awareness merge together this is when your performance can grow exponentially.

Think back to when you are so engrossed in your work that you are in the zone and time and distractions just vanish. When someone interrupting you is annoying. That is flow.

In flow we are more productive, retain more information and our learning increases. We are more creative, innovative, have higher energy and are more likely to collaborate, cooperate and be conscious of ourselves and others. Flow can be heightened working alone or within a team.

Complex problem solving requires intense cognitive focus, so we tend to produce our best and most rewarding work, learn new skills and understand different concepts in positive flow states.

Flow combines five of the most potent neurochemicals the brain can produce and is the only time the brain produces them all at once. WOW, right?!

## What are the other intrinsic benefits of working in flow?

When you are entirely focused on the present and what you're doing, your mind is organised and balanced and this brings about harmony.

In one day, we have over 70,000 thoughts on average running through our heads. That is why deep work and being in a productive state feels good.

There are health benefits as well as productivity ones. The National Institute of Aging found that aside from suppressing productivity and creativity a disorganised mind causes high stress, chronic negativity and impulsivity and can cause serious health issues if prolonged.

I believe this will help you day to day when you need to get creative and particularly when you need to work on your business and strategy. It is why I take myself away to build my strategy each year, why I schedule time to review my business each quarter and again each month on my CEO days. I recreate this environment for my clients with their planning time and hold space in our action intensive sessions too.

So how can you get yourself into a heightened state of flow?

## 1) Batch working

Find a solution for doing the mundane tasks that interrupt your flow and take you into a 'whilst I am here' state. Turn off notifications, create habits to check your email at specific times of the day and decide on the habits you will adopt to address these mundane tasks zapping your time and energy. If you can outsource – do it!

## 2) Manage your distractions

As well as the above, what else is distracting you? What habits do you have that are not serving you? Social media/phones are some of the common distractions.

## 3) Don't multitask

It is a fad that we can. It is the No 1 enemy of flow. Attention is spread too thinly and you absolutely cannot get into a state of flow working this way. This is also the case when you are working and then getting notifications from social media and email. It is not only distracting you, but also means you are spreading yourself too thinly by multitasking.

## 4) Get curious about yourself – how do you work at your best?

What gets you into flow? There are many who say to work for a set period of time before your attention loses focus. This I agree with, but I also think it is unique to you how long you manage to stay focused and how long it takes you to get into flow. I am a good two hours as it takes me a little while to get going and in flow. I don't want to break before I have got there. Others would totally switch off at this point so work out what is right for you. Some say ninety-minute sessions work well. Try it and see.

Consider what distracts you, zaps your productivity, your flow. When you are at your most creative, what is happening internally and externally? What time of the day do you work at your best? Ideally you want to understand what happens to you over a day. Timely is a good app, or you can use a time management spreadsheet to review this.

## 5) What needs to happen to keep you accountable?

Consider how you have stayed accountable to your goals and commitments in the past. What is the right environment for you to get your work done and completed? I facilitate a monthly action intensive session, where they get shit done! It is fascinating to see the impact on productivity when people are in the right environment to flow. The amount you achieve in these small windows when focused is mind-blowing. But what else do you need to stay accountable each day, week and month, so that your boat keeps moving faster?

Workflow and productive behaviour will help you master and protect flow and hence increase your performance.

## How can you take BIG action?

There are many people who will see the goal that they set but fail to take the action they need to achieve it.

Some will see the vision, get excited, but fizzle out before walking the talk. The single greatest key to success is planning plus strategic action!

Without either being executed, the chance of success is significantly lower.

Jon Acuff in *Do Over* says, "Dreaming is fun, future results are enjoyable to talk about. Present efforts are not."

In a previous chapter, I encouraged you to set the sat nav. Now we need to start the car and get driving on your first short journey.

Your car may have the sat nav set, but it also requires fuel.

Your fuel will be your mojo (motivation.) As you know, Simon Sinek is famous for starting with why and it couldn't be relevant than in business. Darren Hardy also gives some brilliant examples of this in his book *The Compound Effect*.

Purpose and why you are doing this are critical.

But don't under-estimate the carrot dangling I talked about in recognition. This is a brilliant way to get yourself emotionally connected to the goal you need to achieve.

What can you do to fuel your tank? It may be a higher purpose, but it could also be about that holiday you want to go on, a course you want to do, a debt you want to clear. Attach it to a goal you have set yourself to give your car a boost of fuel.

Some time ago on my social platforms, I shared a post about watching our football team. Spurs beat Man City 2-0. At the end, I had a conversation with my husband about being 2-0 down in the 85th minute and how the players respond.

Honestly, some players are beat. Others keep going and may find two goals in them or more.

What about you? Are you going to slow down before the finish line or are you going to keep going until the whistle blows?

As a CEO, you know the buck stops with you. If you have a team, they will look to you for inspiration, direction and leadership. You must demonstrate accountability for your actions and your behaviour.

The accountability ladder in figure 2 is a brilliant illustration of this and builds on the discussion in Question 2 regarding your choice of path (you can choose your path of possibility or your path of limitation).

## Figure 2 – Accountability Ladder

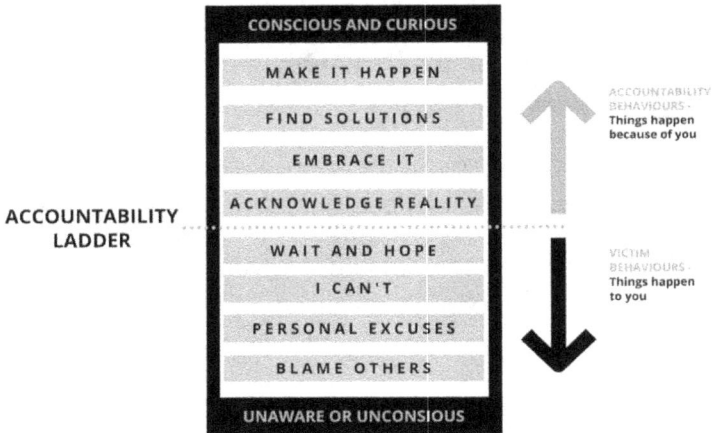

The conscious leader takes accountability and demonstrates accountable behaviours. The unconscious leader demonstrates victim behaviours, apportions blame and doesn't take responsibility.

When pushing for a goal or a result, it is the conscious leader that I urge you to embrace. The one who sees where they need to go, has a clear plan of how they will get there, and takes full responsibility for themselves and their team.

When they arrive at their destination, they take the time to reflect on how the journey went. What went well, what could have gone better, what they have learnt.

Then they get prepared for next time.

This is a conscious leader acting strategically and demonstrating accountability and decisive action.

**Are you ready to become the next generation of CEO? Remember, you have got to move different if you want different.**

---

## Reflections

When were you last in flow? What work were you doing? What do you realise about your work state that puts you in your most productive flow? How are you working? What is your environment like? What time of day do you work best? When are you working? What is/isn't happening? What works well for you that you need to continue? What has stopped you acting in the past? What mostly gets in your way?

### Habits/Distractions

What derails you the most? What zaps your flow? What distracts you the most from taking intentional action? When you sit down to give yourself head space to get creative, to strategise and go all in, what stops you? What triggers do you see that move you from the path of possibility to the path of limitation? How do you typically take action? Are you quick, reflective or do you avoid taking action? How much does this impact your progress?

### Next Steps to the right flow

How could you overcome any negative habits/behaviours that are impacting your workflow and/or decision making right now to create the right productive action taking environment for you?

---

# 10

# WHAT DOES ELEVATION LOOK LIKE?

---

**"Stop shrinking yourself to fit places you've outgrown."**

**"Growth and comfort do not coexist."**

— GINNI ROMETTY

---

W ow! We have done the distance together. If you have made it this far, massive congratulations.

I wrote this book because I wanted to help more business owners like you to grow and realise potential. I believe you have the greatest opportunity in your hands to become part of a new and exciting generation of CEO, but it starts with getting these foundations right to grow from first.

When you lay or re-lay the foundations, you get to create something sustainable in a way that feels aligned for you.

One of my clients who has made some big changes in her already successful business is now seeing some wonderful results. This of course warms my heart, but want to know what warms my heart even more? When she says that her business now feels like it flows, that it is in pure alignment with everything she loves and wants to do. That she is operating from her zone of genius, earning more money, no longer winging it and having more time off. That is what truly warms my heart.

Remember, the journey to becoming a CEO isn't about the title. It never was. You call yourself whatever you choose. But your behaviours, mindset, actions – that is where I urge you to grow.

So, what next?

The foundations in your business are always evolving. That is why the framework is a circle. I want you to check in on yourself and your business on the journey. Dive into the step that is most relevant to where you are. Circumstances change, you evolve, new businesses emerge; you can always go back and review the framework.

When you feel like you have the foundations right with alignment to your product mix, business model, you have strong boundaries and clarity on your strategy, where do you go from here?

Well, you get to decide.

Think back to the vision – what are you ultimately striving for? How far away is the peak of the mountain? What needs to happen for you to reach there?

Your next stage of growth is purely dependent on the stage you are at in your business right now (as outlined in the next generation of CEO) and where you want to go next.

However, for the purpose of our time together, I am going to make some assumptions.

I assume that you are looking to grow and reach more clients by leveraging the time you have available, and that you would like to free up your time and figure out how you can achieve more by doing less. I am also going to assume that you don't want to be working until you hit your grave. Therefore, exiting the business at some point is important to you too.

Elevating to your next level as a leader is a journey I support clients with in my twelve-month high touch, hybrid mastermind and in my leadership 1:1 packages; but to wrap up in here, I have shared some of my further thoughts and insights to reflect on so you can navigate your way from foundations to build phase.

**Your Elevation**

For most, moving to the next level can create new doubts and fear. Remember, confidence comes when you are operating in your comfort zone.

Every time I have stepped up because of a promotion or to a new level in my business, the same sensation comes to say hello. Butterflies in my tummy. The imposter rears its ugly head and pokes me to say, "You really sure you want to do this?"

That is why, as you navigate the next level, you need to be pulled by compelling goals you set yourself that you are emotionally attached to. The formulas that I have shared will really help you to sense check where, if at all, you are holding yourself back.

As you step up, your courage will likely be tested again, your leadership and emotions will need to step up a gear and you will have to (if you haven't already) take the next step of hiring in team support (you may also want to invest in someone externally who can further support your journey). You cannot grow your business alone, nor should you want to.

### What should you consider next?

1. Review your financials to plan as needed for increasing on the VAT threshold and making a move from sole trader to Ltd.
2. Review your business model and look at ways you could scale existing products or add additional products deeper or wider in your model to enable you to scale and leverage your time further.
3. Review your systems, processes and legals. What is causing you a risk that you need to resolve quickly to protect your business? What is slowing you down? What could you automate and streamline to make you more efficient?
4. Review your sales, funnel and marketing strategy – where are your distribution channels right now? Are you positioning yourself right and connecting to enough of your ideal clients to build the audience size you will need to move to the next financial level you have in mind?
5. How could you manage your marketing more strategically and efficiently? What could you do to

repurpose your content and utilise more of these distribution channels?

6. How could you improve your automated funnel set up and build your email list?

7. How are you currently nurturing and building relationships and brand awareness with your audience?

8. Is there a way you could formalise an ambassador programme in your business to bring in additional referrals?

9. Review your operations – are you maximising your customer experience? Is your CRM system sufficient? Where are the gaps in your customer and sales journey and processes?

10. Do you know your statistics and insights? Are you aware of the client retention levels in your business? How could you improve this?

11. How well known are your brand and profile? What needs to change to support your growth? What are all of the customer touch points? Are you happy with them?

12. What are the assets you need to help you with this next phase of growth?

13. What do you struggle with most as a leader? What is currently holding you back from fulfilling your potential?

14. How involved are you in the various functions in your business? What needs to change for you to start to step away from the day-to-day running of your business? What team do you need to bring on to free up your time?

15. Where is your zone of genius and where do you want

to develop it into the future? What would your ideal CEO job spec look and feel like?

16. Who could you hire right now that would free up ten hours of your time?

17. Who could you hire now that could generate revenue into your business and pay for themself?

### You ready for a team?

Hiring is an integral step to your growth. I advocate bringing someone in ahead of 'ready-ness'. I suggest this because it means your growth can be more fluid and your team can help support continuity for your customer experience.

A common question I am asked is, should I hire to my payroll or bring in a freelancer?

Again, this is personal choice. I like to understand the specifics as I don't believe there is a one size fits all approach.

But I will say this. If you hire onto your payroll (in house) it will allow the person to focus solely on your business. There is more to consider legally and in terms of benefits; but it can work out more cost effective to bring someone in house.

It also affords you the luxury of taking them on the journey with you. Investing in their development and rewarding them for their contribution can be rewarding for both of you.

But I will say it again. It is your business. You get to choose what works best for you.

When you hire a freelancer, that doesn't mean you should skip the hiring process. My current strategy is to hire freelancers. But I hire, onboard and integrate a freelancer into my team in the exact way that I would hire someone onto my payroll. I also onboard them and put legal contracts in place for them too. You never need to go legal until you need to go legal. You should plan for the worst and get your roof fixed before the rain again! It is unlikely you'll need it, but it's good to know you won't get wet.

Whether you decide to hire to your payroll or hire freelance, be clear about the support you are looking for to start with. Please don't assume that your first hire needs to be a personal assistant or a VA (virtual assistant). Often it is an admin role that comes first, but it is critical you do the leg work to find out where someone would make the biggest difference to your business right now. Jeff Bezos hired a software developer as his first employee. This was clearly a strategic move!

Whatever person(s) is your first hire, you will need a job description (role and its responsibilities) and an ideal person specification (skills, attributes and personality traits required for the role). Outline the hours you want them to work and the relevant rate of pay for the role. Be clear about what they can expect and gain from being in the role. Talk about your business values and culture and discuss benefits, development opportunities, reporting and team.

Then go out to market to hire. There are several ways you can do this. You could ask in your existing network, you could liaise with universities or colleges if you are prepared to put in the work to develop someone. You could look at anyone you have currently who may be suitable for development. You could enquire on your social media, place an online advert or work with a recruitment company.

Be clear about the interview process and if you do not feel you have the skills to do this effectively, invest in your development or find someone to help you do this right. You want everyone who comes into your space to have a positive experience, irrespective of whether they are the right fit for your business.

Make sure that whoever you bring in, their role frees up time from something you are doing right now and either don't want to be doing, or that someone could do better. Or that you hire someone in to generate revenue for your business and you set them clear KPIs and measure their performance. This way you are leveraging time and adding to your bottom line as part of the investment. Move yourself into your zone of genius as much as possible and fully leverage your strengths. Ultimately, you want to create an organisation that is enabling this through the team too. When you are all leveraging your strengths, you are maximising your energy and performance. Joy really becomes part of your culture.

Be sure that the values are aligned in your hiring process and whatever you do, avoid just getting a bum on a seat. Sometimes when you are in a desperate state or when you interview several people for a role and none of them feel like a fit, you take on the closest match. This isn't a wise move. Ride it out and take the time to find the right person. The wrong unintentional hire can do more harm than good.

When you find your right person, be sure to get contracts in place for them (even if they are a freelancer); be clear on their job role. Do an induction and work hard to onboard them in the right way too. The more time you invest up front, the better fit they will be for you.

Then it is about your leadership. Consciously leading, communicating, delegating, developing and recognising in a way that allows all of the team to bring their best self to work and maximise performance in your business.

Hiring doesn't have to be scary, but it does have to be done right. Give it the time and attention it deserves so you get the right people in place to take with you on this exciting journey. I promise it will pay dividends further down the line.

**I know that hiring for the first time can feel terrifying, so I have created a 'Your First Hire' guide that you may find helpful. Scan the QR code to access.**

# CONCLUSION

---

**"If you want to go fast, go alone. If you want to go far, go together."**

— AFRICAN PROVERB

---

Building foundations is one of the most important steps in a project. They take the weight of the build and provide a critical footing to build from.

The same applies in your business and leadership.

By coming this far with me, you have taken that important first step to explore what your future build needs to stand the test of time, and we have discussed the many challenges and exciting opportunities of business along the way!

Whilst the foundations aren't visible to others, you will know the boundaries you have set yourself, the model that will lead you to the top of the mountain and the values you hold close. This will enable you to surround yourself with others who believe what you believe.

This empowers you to lead from the heart consciously and operate in a state of joy whilst doing things your way.

This isn't fluffy. Big results will come. But they come in a way that feels aligned to you. Trust me when I say, this feels truly amazing.

Thank you for coming on this journey with me to laying foundations that you can LEAD from. It is time to do business YOUR way.

Remember this.

**You are becoming the next generation of CEO.**

**No more winging it.**

**The landscape is officially changed**

# THANK YOU

To you, for taking your precious time to read my very first book. I hope that it has delivered on your expectations and will help make a difference and pave the way forward for your foundations and future success.

To Grahame, Henry and Charlie. We have been through so much together. You rock my world; my heart is full when you are all by my side. You are my why and my reason for creating freedom, so we can continue to create more memories and joy on this crazy journey of life. Thank you for being the wind beneath my wings.

To my Mum and close friends who see behind the scenes. You keep me grounded and remind me to practise what I preach about slowing down to speed up. The honesty, kindness, fun and support that I get to lean in on are forever appreciated.

To my Dad, who showed me early on that running a business of your own can work if you do.

To my wing woman, Lindsey. There are not enough words to express my gratitude for your unwavering support and excellence over the years. You have seen more than most of this journey. You, along with the team that we are developing, enable me to perform in my zone of genius and I am beyond thankful for your support and friendship. I cannot wait to jump into the next chapter together with you by my side.

To my clients – you are the inspiration behind this book. You've trusted me, leaned in on my experience and soaked up everything I have shared. For every student that has been through my Get Set for Success™ Programme I will be forever grateful for your trust. Your feedback has helped me shape and evolve the programme and contribute to this book. You inspire me every single day to do and be more.

To my business buddies. There are too many of you to name. You get it what it is like to ride this crazy journey of business. You help me see that I am not alone. I am eternally grateful for your wisdom, support, laugh out loud moments and friendship. Leaning in never felt so good.

To the mentors, leaders, teachers and educators who have helped shape who I am today – thank you. There are way too many of you to mention for fear of missing someone out. However, I would especially like to thank Abigail Horne and the incredible team at Authors and Co for making this book a reality; I got there in the end! Thank you for helping me bring it to life. A giant thanks to Phil Jones who picked me up at one of my lowest points on this bonkers journey of business and saw my potential when I doubted it most. You remain generous to this day and inspire me more than you'll ever know; thank you just doesn't seem enough. To Lisa Johnson and Jade Gemma, you were the push I needed to bring Get Set for

Success™ to life and I will be forever grateful. For every other mentor and coach who has and continues to guide and hold space for me, I thank you. Every single one of you has played a part in my leadership journey and helped bring to life this book.

Finally. Thank you to me. For sticking through the dark times, not quitting when it felt too hard. You stayed curious, open minded and continued to challenge the status quo. I have realised it really is ok to dream bigger, to zig when others zag and do things YOUR way. I am proud to have proved the nay-sayers wrong and to champion others to do the same.

# REFERENCE AND RECOMMENDATIONS

I am a lifelong learner, book worm and my knowledge (and library) grows daily.

I want to draw your attention to the following authors and organisations whom I have referenced (and highly recommend) in this book.

Phil M Jones
Exactly What to Say

Gay Hendricks
The Big Leap

Daniel Priestley
Oversubscribed

Marcus Sheridan
They Ask, You Answer

Mike Michalowicz
Profit First

Debra Corey
Bringing Values out to Play

Strengthscope®

Andrew Bryant and Ana Kanzan
Self Leadership

Jim Dethmer, Diana Chapman, Kaley Klemp
15 Commitments to Conscious Leadership

Darren Hardy
The Compound Effect

# MEET THE AUTHOR

Leigh Howes is a qualified Executive Coach specialising in leadership and business coaching, mentoring and consultancy support to service-based businesses. With over 20 years' experience in partnering and advising high performing business leaders (including to board level within a Fortune500), she has cultivated hundreds of leaders to embrace change, elevate performance and realise their potential.

Passionate about holding a safe and stretching space, Leigh advocates a 'me-first' approach, encouraging a more balanced outlook to life. She believes there is an incredible opportunity within business models today to work smarter, with greater consciousness of and alignment to what matters most. She unapologetically shines a light on embracing leadership and achieving higher levels of performance without working around the clock.

Leigh has the gift of being able to read people and see beneath the surface of what holds them back. It's this, coupled with her vast knowledge, supportive style and honest feedback that has led to many ambitious business leaders wanting her in their corner supporting their next stage of growth.

instagram.com/leighahowes

linkedin.com/in/leighhowes1

facebook.com/growwithleigh

KIND WORDS

"Helping one person might not change the world; but it could change the world for one person."

"Before working with Leigh, business was good, but I was falling into the trap of working too much and having less and less time with my family. The support has given me the confidence to make some big changes, even when it would have been safer to carry on doing things the way I was before."

— **REBECCA WISE – CEO & FUNNEL STRATEGIST**

"If you need a good kick up the behind, Leigh will go find her boots. Leigh can help you untangle your myriad of business ideas and help mould them into a viable business model."

— **MICHELLE ESHKERI – CEO & COPYWRITER**

"I cannot recommend working with Leigh enough – it's like having a cheerleader, guru and mind-reader in your pocket."

— **ANNA WATSON – CEO & SALES CONSULTANT**

# ADDITIONAL RESOURCES

## JOIN LEIGH ON FACEBOOK

Get direct access to Leigh and more tips and support in her free private book members' community. Give the private book readers' code MYWAY upon entry.

*www.facebook.com/groups/foundationstoleadfrom*

## BUSINESS YOUR WAY – BITE SIZED TRAINING

A great next step from this book is Leigh's bite sized sixty-minute self-study training (with workbook). Leigh shares more of her knowledge and experience so you can take steps to design a business model that 100% fits you. In this low cost, high impact session she will touch on your own 'must haves', non-negotiable boundaries, time leveraging and pricing strategies - inspiring you to take further action to maximise your happiness, fulfilment and performance.

*www.leighhowes.com/business-your-way*

## GET SET FOR SUCCESS – THE PROGRAMME

Leigh's six-month online development programme changes the way business owners lead themselves and their businesses. Walking you through her foundations framework and going deeper on the topics she discusses in this book, Leigh gives you additional support in a private community and direct access to Leigh herself. This programme aims to get you accountable to develop the foundations in your business. The programme is available in live and digital self-study versions.

*www.leighhowes.com/get-set-for-success*

## JOIN LEIGH IN HER PRIVATE MEMBERS' LOUNGE

Leigh recognises that investing in yourself early on in your journey of self-development can feel daunting. That is why The Business Leaders' Lounge is the perfect place to start. Pay monthly or annually and get support, community, networking, training, members directory and a monthly group support call with Leigh. This supports your development, gets you amongst like-minded peers, and gives you a taster of what it is like to have Leigh in your corner.

*www.leighhowes.com/business-leaders-lounge*

# FIND OUT HOW YOU CAN WORK DIRECTLY WITH LEIGH

Discover how you (and your team) can work closely with Leigh in her intimate mastermind group or privately 1-to-1.

*www.leighhowes.com/work-with-me*

# BOOK LEIGH TO SPEAK TO YOUR COMMUNITIES OR AT YOUR EVENT

Get Leigh to be your next inspiring and dynamic speaker or trainer. Fun, engaging and inspiring, Leigh can pack a punch when it comes to delivering a training, talk or presentation to inspire a change in thinking and behaviour and to help change the landscape and create our next generation of CEOs and Leaders.

***Contact Leigh's team at*** *hello@leighhowes.com*